Wise Guys

A Guide to Building Godly Character in Boys

by Dan and Carol Fiddler

BACK TO THE BIBLE
Publishing

WISE GUYS
published by Back to the Bible Publishing
Copyright © 2001 by Dan and Carol Fiddler
International Standard Book Number 0-8474-5406-1

Photography: Kimberly Slaughter Photography
Technical support: Digimatrix—Medford, Oregon

The Bible text used in this publication, unless otherwise noted, is from the HOLY BIBLE: NEW INTERNATIONAL VERSION®. Copyright © 1973, 1978, 1984 by International Bible Society. Used by permission of Zondervan Publishing House.
Use of italics in Bible texts is added by the authors for emphasis.
The Bible text designated as NKJV in this publication is from the HOLY BIBLE: NEW KING JAMES VERSION®. Copyright © 1979, 1980, 1982 by Thomas Nelson, Inc. Used by permission.

For information:
Back to the Bible
P.O. Box 82808
Lincoln, NE 68501
www.backtothebible.org

1 2 3 4 5 6 7—05 04 03 02 01

Printed in the USA

Foreword

In the early 1980s, while living in New York City, I encountered a teenage boy on a subway who had just been stabbed in his chest with a knife. While he screamed for his life, a few of us adults found a place for him to lie down. With blood pouring from his chest, his eyes began to dilate. There was great panic, hysteria and noise from the bystanders. As a new Christian, I knelt down next to the boy and offered him the only significant words I knew. I told him that God loved him. All of a sudden those out-of-control eyes stared hopefully at me, and he asked, "He does?"

Since that compelling episode I have concluded that yes, teenage boys will respond to the passionate, loving call of the Lord Jesus Christ. Thankfully, most youngsters won't experience a sudden, violent death, yet many teenage boys are dying a slow death apart from a relationship with Jesus.

While reading *Wise Guys*, I was moved with conviction and a renewed sense of compassion for our teenage boys. *Wise Guys* presents a direct, practical, yet passionate plea for young men in their unique challenges and temptations to be Joseph-like, Daniel-like, David-like and, most important, Jesus-like difference-makers.

Dan and Carol Fiddler have skillfully presented numerous references from God's Word with relevant examples pertaining to teenage boys that are easy to understand. Whether you are a teenager, a college football coach like myself, or anyone of either gender who has a heart to see teenage boys become champions for Christ, you will be inspired by *Wise Guys*!

— *Ron Brown*

Assistant Football Coach, University of Nebraska, Lincoln
Host of the weekly radio program *Going the Distance*
and Cohost of the radio program *The Voice of Mission Nebraska*

Contents

A Word to Parents

From Carol

Maybe you're wondering why we chose this title or if it's a joke. We have received differing reactions to the title, and we hope that this explanation will help to clarify its meaning for you.

"Wise men" of all sorts have been called upon throughout history to solve problems, provide answers to mysteries and give interpretations and wisdom to leaders. But there were and are some genuinely wise guys who recognize their limitations, their need for God and their dependence on Him for and in everything.

When you look through the Bible you see a distinction between the world's wisdom and godly wisdom. Throughout the Word, God rebukes and mocks the so-called wise men who do not seek counsel from Him. A story in 1 Samuel 5 illustrates the folly of misguided wisdom. The Philistines had captured the ark of the Lord, brought it from Israel to their home country and set it up as a trophy in the temple of their "god" Dagon. When the Philistines saw for themselves that the God of Israel was more powerful than their god, Dagon did a face plant before the ark.

The next day Dagon repeated the face plant, this time with a triple twist—both its hands and head were broken off and a mere stump remained. The Philistines asked their "wisest men" (priests, rulers and diviners) what to do. These "wise men" saw that this God was clearly real and obviously greater than their god, but they preferred to remain in their own comfort zone of worship. Rather than bow the knee and desire to know this powerful God, they sent Him packing. Back to Israel He went, while they resumed their status quo: worship of a dead statue. What a tragic outcome of an encounter with God! The "wise men" said, "Get God out of here so we can resume our lives."

There were other "wise guys," however, who heard that there was a new King in Israel, a Lord greater than their lords. These guys demonstrated true wisdom in dropping everything, packing themselves up (with gifts to give) and going the distance to find Him and worship Him. The Magi didn't know all there was to know about this Jesus, but they followed their hearts and allowed God to direct them step-by-step. The contrast is clear. Real wise men will seek Jesus. Real wise men will go to the ends of the earth to find Him. Real wise guys are ready for change in their lives when they encounter the Lord. Real wise guys will humbly bow their knee to the King of kings and Lord of lords!

Living in a secular world, our sons will choose which kind of wise men to become. There was a man who stood out as an excellent example, living as a wise man in a worldly environment. Daniel was counted among Babylon's wise men. There he was, a true lover of God, in an extremely worldly place. You know his story. His commitment to honor God above all else gave validity to his wisdom, and as he sought answers from God, His wisdom was found superior to all others.

True wise guys know that wisdom is a gift from God. This is our desire for all young men—that they be found truly wise because they have sought the wisdom of the Lord in every area of their lives. We pray that God is raising up a generation of real wise guys!

From Dan

In the course of obtaining my education, our family has crisscrossed the country. Carol and I have had the pleasure of living in the Chicago area, in wonderful university towns in North Carolina and Iowa and, for the last nine years, in Oregon. Along the way on this coast-to-coast tour we have participated in youth and children's ministries in many different churches in a variety of denominations.

Over the years, we have developed strong friendships with numerous Christian families involved in business, education, athletics and many other vocational pursuits. One consistent trend many of these families noted is a decline in personal character issues in Christian kids raised in Christian families who are part of Bible-believing churches. For example, Christian businessmen note that they used to be able to depend on Christian teens as employees, but now it is common to find a marginal work ethic in "churched" kids. The integrity and responsibility they used to be able to count on is now just as rare to find in Christians as it is among secular teens.

Educators comment on their surprise at the defiant attitudes and actions of Christians in both public and Christian schools. There is a lack of character among such students, but there is no shortage of Christian students who are "real characters." Coaches as well as parents cringe over Christian athletes who display behavior towards their teammates, opponents and officials that could be described as anything but Christlike. We know our kids are sinners (they were born to us, after all), but we also know that we are not called to be conformed to this world but to be transformed—metamorphosed—by the renewing of the mind (Romans 12:2). We are to be conformed to the image of His Son (Romans 8:29), not to the image the world has put before our sons as the quintessential American male: rugged, fiercely independent, pleasure-seeking and above all, cool and popular.

It is beyond question that this transformation is a lifelong process; nobody expects spiritual perfection by junior high. However, it is my contention that with the Lord's help, much of the character-building process can be accomplished in the home, and the preteen years present a golden opportunity for growth in character. Sociologists tell us that by the time our sons reach high school, more of their learning and input comes from peers than from parents. Parents still have input, obviously, but the peer group has greater influence, a louder voice than mom or dad.

As a parent, that leads me to two important conclusions. First, in the junior high and high school years, I better have a good idea who is in my son's circle of tight friends, because they will influence him. Second, this compels me to take advantage of the opportunity to have spiritual input in these preteen years, when his intellect is capable of discussing and understanding important concepts and his influence switch is still pointed more towards parents than peers.

It is also abundantly clear that there is no magical formula parents can follow to guarantee spiritual growth in our kids, nor can we claim credit for spiritual life that is present. Any growth that takes place is from the Lord, not from us. As Paul puts it in 1 Corinthians 3:6, "I planted the seed, Apollos watered it, but God made it grow." So if God brings about the growth, what responsibility do we have? We can plant seeds of faith in the young men God has entrusted to us; we can water with the Word in generous amounts; we can surround them with the warmth of the Son in their immediate environment. In short, we can let the Lord use us in the process of spiritual growth towards godliness.

This book is our hearts' passion for our kids. We present it as those who are working through the process ourselves, not as a family that has mastered every page or concept included in this work. Much of it is a compilation of discussions Carol and I have had over the Word both with our children and between ourselves. I am deeply indebted to my wife for her initiative and desire to put together such a tool for others. If the writing depended entirely on me, these pages would still be blank.

We pray that this book will be useful to your family as the Lord brings about growth in your son, that he may be "like a tree planted by streams of water, which yields its fruit in season and whose leaf does not wither. Whatever he does prospers" (Psalm 1:3).

Introduction

"Who wants to play Bible Trivia?" I asked one night in our grade school class. Dan had finished the Bible teaching and we were ready to play games until the service was over. Quite a few kids wanted to play Bible Trivia that night, and I decided to start with the easy questions to give them a boost. Question after question was asked. I kept going through the cards, asking the easiest questions I could find, but no one could answer them! I was puzzled and heartbroken. These were the children who *wanted* to play the game. That implied they had a little Bible knowledge. The words of Hosea came back to me in a haunting way: "'My people are destroyed from lack of knowledge'" (Hosea 4:6). The prophet was declaring that it was God's people, not the heathens, who no longer knew Him.

I used to wonder how this could be. That night in our children's class, the reality of this truth hit me harder than ever. We live in a time in which the heritage of God and His ways is not being passed on to the younger generation in a majority of Christian homes. Maybe this indicates a lack of hunger and thirst for righteousness even in the lives of parents. True hunger and thirst are filled. That's the promise of Matthew 5:6. If parents are filled, they cannot help but spill it over to their children. Maybe the lack of discipling of today's kids is a result of living in a society that is always on the go and out of balance. Parents are too rushed to sit and discuss the Word of God even though it has the answers to all of life. Or perhaps the problem is a perceived lack of know-how.

For a variety of reasons, many children are coming up bankrupt in the category of knowing God and walking in His ways. This has resulted in a wavering in character. That's why we offer this book as a tool for both parent and child to see how applicable God's Word is to everyday life and the issues of life. It is a guide you can use to get your son "plugged in" to the Word of God in a way that will help shape his character while familiarizing him with some of the great stories in the Bible and their spiritual significance. It is, we admit, quite meaty. There is a lot to chew on, contemplate and incorporate into one's life here. It may require some digestion on the parent's part first before diving into it with his or her son. It might be better for a father or mother to read through the lesson, divide it into smaller digestible chunks and share it with his son even without the book in hand. Each parent will find the way to best approach his or her son, depending on the boy's foundation in the Bible.

"When your words came, I ate them; they were my joy and my heart's delight" (Jeremiah 15:16). Jeremiah's declaration about God's Word is a concept of feeding on God's Word as a regular, essential and indispensable part of life so that we are nourished and strengthened. We parents need to be the catalyst that develops this type of spiritual appetite in our kids.

Our kids also need to thirst for the Living Water, Jesus Christ. He alone can satisfy; He alone can keep us on the right path. Our kids desperately need the solid food of the Word (Hebrews 5:14) in order to become *thinkers*, able to process the Word of God as it relates to the culture in which we live. They need to be students of the Word so that they may have "an answer to everyone who asks the reason for the hope that you have" (1 Peter 3:15).

The lack of knowledge of God will someday be reversed, so that the entire earth will be full of this knowledge, "'as the waters cover the sea,'" says Habakkuk 2:14. While this prophecy speaks of the millennial kingdom, the concept can be true for you and your family today: your earthly sphere, your family, can be filled to overflowing with the knowledge of the glory of the Lord. Think of the difference this could make if every true believer would fill his or her home with heartfelt love and knowledge of God! This foundation is to be the tool God's Holy Spirit uses to guide and direct each member of your family into a meaningful, purposeful and personal relationship with Him. The Holy Spirit takes the knowledge we obtain and makes it life-giving sustenance for our daily life.

This book is designed to be a partnership of parent and child discovering together God's heart for spiritual growth and the development of godly character. It is our prayer that this will be a tool the Lord will use to "'turn the hearts of the fathers to their children, and the hearts of the children to their fathers'" (Malachi 4:6). We pray that together, the hearts of parents and their boys will be compelled to grow in a deeper love for God and His ways, which are perfect.

"My soul yearns, even faints, for the courts of the LORD; my heart and my flesh cry out for the living God" (Psalm 84:2).

"I have treasured the words of his mouth more than my daily bread" (Job 23:12).

The Bible tells us to work hard at pursuing godly qualities.

Character Building

"A good name is more desirable than great riches."
Proverbs 22:1

"The man of integrity walks securely, but he who takes crooked paths will be found out."
Proverbs 10:9

Are you a young man of character, or simply a "character"? So what's the big deal about character anyway? "I already have plenty of character," you might say. "I'm the 'life of the party' with my friends." Perhaps this is all you think of when you hear the word *character*. Maybe it is an unfamiliar word and the only way you've heard it used is when an adult talks about the attention-grabbing behavior of a child. Its original meaning has been forgotten. This book will reintroduce you to the word *character*, redefine it and, hopefully, surprise you with how broad and deep its meaning is.

The Bible gives a mandate (an order or command) to the Christian to pursue good character and godliness so that he will be happy and blessed. That's another reason to take the challenge: God *wants* you to be happy. Not only does good character make the believer's life better, but it also makes his life a great testimony and witness for God. Throughout the New Testament are lists of qualities that you are to be working into your life so that you will be solid in your faith and upright in your living. This effort will keep you from being blown away by life's problems.

Not only does good character make the believer's life better, but it also makes his life a great testimony and witness for God.

One such list of godly character qualities is in 2 Peter 1:5–7. This passage tells every believer to diligently work on building the qualities of moral excellence, knowledge, self-control, perseverance, godliness, brotherly kindness and love into his life. And, it comes with a fantastic promise. It says that if you as a Christian live out these qualities, you will not be useless or unfruitful and will not stumble. What an awesome promise! Putting your energy into developing these qualities will give you a great advantage in life.

It has been said that character is who you are when no one is looking. When you get to correct your own work in school, are you tempted to pass over a question you know you answered wrong?

What do you do with that temptation? If answers to a test were out on the teacher's desk, would you glance at them to see if you could get some of the answers? If someone left his basketball on the school playground, would it be reasonable to take it home? These are issues of integrity and character.

"Ouch!" you say. "That's too close to home." True, but issues of the heart need to be looked at regularly and reworked. It can hurt sometimes, but growing pains are not just physical. They are also spiritual. Remember that the Bible says when a person is in Christ, he is a new creature (2 Corinthians 5:17). Putting off your old, undesirable traits also means putting on new, great qualities. Take the challenges of this book, practice them, and you'll like the finished product—that's a promise!

Character is also the collection of traits and qualities within an individual. Each person has a combination of good and bad traits in him. There are good traits that are to be steadily developed, as well as flaws and weaknesses that are to be corrected. The Bible tells us to work hard at pursuing godly qualities (1 Timothy 6:11 and 2 Timothy 2:22). A person who is known as having good character has established a good reputation for himself based on what others have seen of his actions and attitudes. This reputation is based on the way he treats others and the way he handles himself. That does not mean he never struggles in difficult situations. Good character does not come easily. It is achieved through the continual practice of making good choices in daily situations. This includes what a person does with the thoughts that enter his mind and what he chooses to do with his free time when no one else is around. Developing good character requires hard work, but the payoff in the end is great: *people know they can trust and count on a person of good character*.

Over time a person of good character does well because he does not hesitate in choosing right over wrong in tough situations. There is no compromise in his life. He has decided that truth must rule in all situations. He understands he is to put others first, above his own desires. He chooses to show love and respect for all people. He knows it's not okay to keep something he found until he's made every effort to find its owner. He replaces something borrowed that he has lost or broken. Why? Because he understands that he should build into his life absolute standards of honesty and uprightness by practice and diligence. Through this he will become a more solid, complete and dependable person.

This, of course, was God's plan for all of humanity from the beginning. He wanted all people to live by His standards because He knew what was best, what would make people happy and what would keep society running smoothly.

It's a lot easier in the short run to decide you don't care about your growth and then run your life the way you think it should go. But God's Word says there will be losses for living in that kind of pride. The Bible says that you can count on reaping what you sow (Galatians 6:7–9). That means there are real consequences for the choices you make. When you make good choices (sowing), there will be good rewards (reaping), though not always immediate. You may be tempted at times to think that you are a "special case," free from a biblical principle. Maybe you believe certain principles apply only to other people but not to you. This twisted thinking is not from God and is dangerous. The truth is, when you make choices against God's principles, there will be damage to your soul. Sometimes these consequences for wrong choices are slow in coming, but be assured, they will come. The biblical principle of reaping what you sow is a *protection* to keep you from continuing in harmful sin.

As you study this book you will learn about godly qualities and how you are to work them into your life. As you look at their life stories, you will see how men before you built godliness into their lives. You also will look at some men who made bad choices and see the frustrations they experienced because of choosing the wrong path. Every story will challenge you to work on building godly character into your life. Adding these characteristics to your life will cause you to become a true "wise guy."

Don't Forget It 👉 *(answers on page 121)*

1. Good character is developed through making good choices in _____ decisions.

2. My personal good character is a benefit to others because they can _____ me.

3. God promises to bless my determination to work on godliness by making my life _____.

4. I have good traits to develop as well as _____ in my life, which need to be corrected.

Further Study

We can be *taught* many good things about good character. But good character is best developed through the tests, challenges and temptations we go through and by the many choices we make each day. Study Joseph's life from this outlook (Genesis 37, 39–50). Joseph's good character was shown most clearly by his reactions when people wronged him. Notice and discuss Joseph's constant hard work no matter where he was (in the pit, the prison or the palace), his commitment to rightness, his ability to resist temptation and his kindness and forgiveness towards his brothers. All of these qualities show Joseph's incredible trust in God *no matter what happened in his life*. He would not be brought low by the situations of life. Read what Romans 5:1–5 says about difficulties in life producing character and perseverance in us.

Look through the following passages for other qualities God desires Christians to work on. Most lists have a combination of good and bad traits as a contrast.

Romans 12:9–18

Galatians 5:19–23

Ephesians 4:31–32 and 5:1–7

Colossians 3:5–14

1 Timothy 6:11

Titus 2:6–8

1 Peter 3:8–9

Notes

_____

_____

_____

_____

_____

Obedience requires faith when instructions don't make sense to you.

Life's Key

"'Be strong and very courageous. Be careful to obey all the law my servant Moses gave you; do not turn from it to the right or to the left, that you may be successful wherever you go. Do not let this Book of the Law depart from your mouth; meditate on it day and night, so that you may be careful to do everything written in it. Then you will be prosperous and successful.'"
Joshua 1:7–8

With seven seconds left in the basketball game, Tyler's team was down one point, and Coach Wilson called a time out. While the coach was mapping out the play for the last shot, Tyler was annoyed that he wasn't picked to take the shot. He was a good clutch player, had the highest shooting percentage on the team and was a great three-point shooter, but this time the coach chose Nick, the tallest on the team, for a layup. Rather than setting the screen he was supposed to, Tyler pulled out, hoping to get a quick pass and shoot the three. The in-bounds man, now unable to get the ball in to Nick, desperately threw it to Tyler. Tyler's shot bounced in and out, the defense rebounded, the clock ran out and the game was lost. In this situation, Tyler decided he knew better than the coach and was going to prove it to everyone. Instead, Tyler's disrespect for the coach and his directions led to frustration and disappointment for the whole team.

Following directions can lead to great breakthroughs in turning a game around or pushing ahead.

In any game situation, when a coach calls a play for a team to follow, everyone has a choice to make—to follow through with the plan or not. What happens when one guy doesn't follow it? There is no advancement or scoring. In fact, it usually sets the team back and allows the other team to advance and score. Following directions can lead to great breakthroughs in turning a game around or pushing ahead. In contrast, one person's disregard of instructions can lead to disaster for the whole team.

The Israelites found themselves in a similar situation. The first battle recorded in the Book of Joshua—the battle of Jericho—is well known. It is an amazing story because God's directions wouldn't have *made sense* to the Israelites. How could they conquer a city by marching around it? The Israelites learned an important lesson during that week of marching around Jericho: *following God's instruction exactly brings victory and blessing*. If the Israelites had decided that because

God's directions didn't make sense to them they should fight the battle the way they thought it was supposed to be fought, there would have been great losses. This generation had never fought a battle before and they were inexperienced. Many of their own men would have died in battle, and the Israelites might have even been defeated and become slaves again. The blessing they received from obeying God's direction was *life*! Not needing to fight a battle spared their energy and supplies. This left them strong for the next task.

Think about the spiritual picture here. Every time a Christian chooses to follow his own understanding over God's directions, it costs him greatly and leaves him exhausted, if not defeated. Following one's own way is prideful and exposes a Christian to the possibility of becoming stuck in sin, which will bring trouble and hurt him. Living according to the pattern of God's Word, however, brings God's best blessings to us: peace and a right relationship with Him.

It is no mistake that when Israel began entering the Promised Land, God gave specific directions that would make them successful. You need to understand that God *wanted* Israel to be successful. This was new territory for them and they didn't know the best or right way to approach the people already living there. God repeated His directions with the command to obey *all* of them so that they would have success. The Israelites' obedience to God's instructions would determine their success (or lack of it).

Do you want to have success in life? It requires a determination to follow the Expert's directions. Follow God's counsel, for He is the Expert in regard to all the important issues of life. He has given directions in the Bible because He wants the best for you. Your obedience to His Word will make your life successful by God's standards. That's God's promise to you.

Obedience requires faith. Each choice of obedience to God's Word builds your trust in God. Be careful not to justify disobedience just because His instructions don't make sense to you. Will you commit to follow God's ways to the best of your ability? What instructions are hard for you to follow? What causes you to doubt? Doubt often comes because God's ways are so different from the world's ways of handling a situation. Think about this direction from Proverbs 15:1: "A gentle answer turns away wrath, but a harsh word stirs up anger." Have you seen what happens when you respond to your brother or sister with angry and mean words? What kind of reaction do you get?

God says that your gentle reply will cool a heated situation. Try it and you'll see that your obedience to God's instruction works.

"As for God, his way is perfect; the word of the LORD is flawless. He is a shield for all who take refuge in him" (Psalm 18:30).

Don't Forget It 👉 *(answers on page 121)*

1. My _____ to God's instructions determines my spiritual success in life.

2. It takes _____ to obey God's ways when they don't make sense to me.

3. Following my own way over God's way is _____.

Further Study 📖

Proverbs 3:5–6 says we are to trust in the Lord with our whole heart and not lean on our own understanding. Think through the following instructions from God, which are so different from popular thinking. They require faith and trust in God. Discuss how obeying and following God's way will bless your life, make things run more smoothly for you and help your life bless other people too.

Mark 10:43: "'Whoever wants to become great among you must be your servant.'"

Acts 20:35: "'The Lord Jesus himself said: "It is more blessed to give than to receive."'"

Matthew 16:25: "'For whoever wants to save his life will lose it, but whoever loses his life for me will find it.'"

Matthew 5:44: "'Love your enemies and pray for those who persecute you.'"

Titus 3:1–2: "Remind the people to be subject to rulers and authorities, to be obedient, to be ready to do whatever is good, to slander no one, to be peaceable and considerate, and to show true humility toward all men."

Proverbs 22:4: "Humility and the fear of the LORD bring wealth and honor and life."

Ephesians 6:1: "'Honor your father and mother'—which is the first commandment with a promise—'that it may go well with you and that you may live long on the earth.'"

People will look at your life and see God shining through when you obey Him and act in love. The different events and circumstances of your life are the stage upon which God's power, love and kindness are shown to all who observe your life. Your obedience to God's ways will also bless you personally.

Notes

It's important that your closest friends are like-minded about following Jesus and standing up for what is right.

Companions

"He who walks with the wise grows wise, but a companion of fools suffers harm."
Proverbs 13:20

He almost blew it all! Of course, he didn't realize at the time that he was jeopardizing his life-long dream and career goal. Growing up in the slums of Detroit and living at poverty level with his hard-working mother, Ben wanted to fit into a new school more than ever. He was teased continually for not having the "right" clothes. He wanted to fit in with the "in crowd" so desperately that finally, after weeks of pleading, his mother was able to save enough money to buy him a few fashionable clothes. The result of fitting in meant Ben was accepted by the "popular" guys and invited to all their parties. Soon after, however, his grades fell because he allowed his friends to have so much influence on his life. But that was okay with him at the time because he was finally "one of the guys."

As Ben's mother kept reminding him of his dream of being a doctor, he began to realize that he was trapped. He was in a downward spiral of needing to act and live like these new friends in order to keep up with them and stay in their group. His striving to remain a part of this group was unending. Eventually, Ben came to understand that this wrong focus had caused him to walk away from everything that was important to him. It took some time, but Ben got back on track. He decided to let his long-term goal of becoming a doctor (which required lots of studying) rule over the temporary goal of being popular and accepted.

Now as a world-famous neurosurgeon, Dr. Ben Carson has pioneered many new techniques in brain surgery and changed the lives of many people who had no hope of surviving terminal illnesses. Imagine how his life would have turned out if he had decided that being accepted by "friends" was more important than his life goal! In his early high school years, he became so focused on one thing—the wrong thing—that it almost changed the direction of his whole life. Ben Carson came close to sacrificing his goal of becoming a doctor in order to fit in and be approved by others.

The desire to be a part of the "in crowd" can cause people to make many dangerous compromises, which can have serious effects on your life. The guys you choose to hang out with can have a powerful influence on you. You have probably heard of the term "peer pressure." This is the pressure you feel to do what others are doing so that you will be accepted. It can be tempting to want to please friends and to want to be liked above all else.

Friendship works two ways. You have the opportunity to be a great influence on your friends. Your friends also have a definite influence on you. True friends need to understand right priorities, have respect for each other and help each other succeed in doing what is right. You should not feel a desperate need to be able to do certain things, dress in a certain way or own what is new and popular in order to be accepted.

True friends need to understand right priorities, have respect for each other and help each other succeed in doing what is right.

The Bible defines the root of negative peer pressure perfectly when talking about the rulers of Jesus' day. Many of them believed in Him but were afraid to speak out about Him because of the power of the Pharisees to take away their position. In other words, these men weren't willing to say they believed in Jesus because the Pharisees—their peers, the guys they spent time with in the synagogue—might kick them out. They realized that declaring their faith in Jesus was putting their important positions at risk. This statement in John 12:43 exposes the heart of the issue: these rulers loved the approval or praise of men *more* than they loved the praise of God. This is a sobering way to understand many situations in which you find yourself. Many daily decisions you make come down to the question of how badly you want the approval of your friends. Would you sacrifice the approval of God to get the approval of your friends?

Luke 2:52 tells us that as a 12-year-old, Jesus "grew in wisdom and stature, and in favor with God and men." Notice the order of priority indicated in this verse. It is no coincidence that the Bible records Jesus as growing in favor with God first, before favor with men. Jesus pleased His Father, God, as first priority. Many men didn't like Jesus. Men desiring godliness and men who realized their need for what Jesus had to offer in truth and forgiveness did like Him. Jesus continually chose to work and act in ways that showed His determination to seek the approval of His Father over the approval of mankind. Jesus Himself said, "The one who sent me is with me; he has not left me alone, *for I always do what pleases him*" (John 8:29).

Don't forget about God when you're with your friends. He wants to be an active part of everything you do; He is with you at all times. Jesus' attitude of doing all things to please His Heavenly Father is one you need to have as you go to school, play sports and hang out with friends.

Many times you will be with friends who don't believe in Jesus or want to follow Him. These are times for you to be strong in your faith and be a positive influence on them. The question is, "Are you (your behavior, attitudes and values) rubbing off on them, or are they (their behavior, attitudes and values) rubbing off on you? The answer to this question is a good indication of how much time you should spend around certain friends. The saying "just say no" says it all. You don't need to say anything more—no apologies or excuses. If that is too difficult for you, separate yourself from friendships in which it is too hard for you to make good choices.

People assume you to be like the guys you spend time with. It is important that your closest friends are like-minded about following Jesus and standing up for what is right. You are probably very familiar with a story about three friends who stood together through a fiery trial, Hananiah, Mishael and Azariah, also known as Shadrach,

Meshach and Abednego. Do you know that their very good friend was Daniel? When King Nebuchadnezzar had a dream that no "wise man" could interpret, he ordered that all the wise men in his court be put to death (Daniel 2). Daniel understood how deadly this situation was. He had the courage to go by himself directly to the king and ask for time to interpret the dream. Then he went to his friends, Hananiah, Mishael and Azariah, and asked for their help in praying with him to "plead for mercy from the God of heaven" (Daniel 2:18). He asked them to support him in prayer, that God would reveal the secret of the dream. This is the kind of friendship you want to begin to develop early in life—the type you can call on for support and encouragement.

Out of all the young men from Israel who were carried to Babylon as prisoners, these four are the only ones written about who still followed and honored God. Daniel and his friends needed to support and encourage each other to remain faithful in that foreign land filled with godlessness. This is like the world you live in today. It may seem like there are few around you who love God. It may seem like a lonely world for you. You need a friend or two who will support and help you as you grow up and live for God. Ask the Lord to show you those who can be the right kind of friends or companions for you, that together you will be known as ones who please God rather than please people. Paul put it this way in Galatians 1:10: "If I were still trying to please men, I would not be a servant of Christ."

Daniel, Hananiah, Mishael and Azariah were loyal friends. They understood that true friendship meant holding each other responsible for strong character traits such as truthfulness, respect and integrity. They also understood that good friends pray for each other and encourage each other.

Good friendships have give and take. Be sure that you choose good friends and look for ways to build up and encourage each other.

"Let us consider how we may spur one another on toward love and good deeds" (Hebrews 10:24).

Don't Forget It ☞ *(answers on page 121)*

1. True friends help each other do what is _____.

2. There is great danger in wanting the approval of _____ more than the approval of God.

3. Good friends will hold each other responsible for _____ character.

4. "If I were still trying to please men, I would not be a _____ of Christ."

Further Study 📖

The influence of peers is powerful. The story of Daniel shows that peers can be a great support and help to each other. There is also an illustration in the Bible of the dangers of peer influence. In 1 Kings 12:6–14, Rehoboam, the new king of Israel, sought advice on how to best govern the people. He first consulted the elders who had been a help to his father, King Solomon. These men had the benefit of watching Solomon rule the Israelites, and they could see what mistakes he had made. That's the wisdom and insight that comes with the age and experience of those who are older. These men gave Rehoboam solid advice that would have caused the people of Israel to willingly serve and support him as their king.

But Rehoboam then asked "the young men" (v. 8), peers his own age, what they would do in this situation, and the result was disaster and rebellion. These young "advisors" were inexperienced and lacked understanding of good leadership. They suggested harsh labor and cruel discipline. The great mistake Rehoboam made is that he "rejected the advice the elders gave him" (v. 8). It's not that young people cannot give good advice. In fact, many young people have great vision and unique ideas that are inspirational. However, advice from peers or elders always needs to be checked with the truths of God's principles to see if it is consistent with His nature and His standards. It is important to value what older people have learned in their lifetime; it can prevent many mistakes.

Read John 5:44 and 1 Thessalonians 2:4–6, and note situations in your life that cause you to want to be honored before others. Pray that God would show you how to please Him in those situations. Verses regarding friends and companions include Proverbs 2:20–22, Proverbs 14:7 and Psalm 1:1. These verses address the issue of the kind of people with whom you spend the majority of your time. Notice that Psalm 1:1 warns against time spent walking, standing and sitting with the ungodly. Friendliness to all is important, but companionship is another matter and must be considered carefully. King Herod committed a great sin in ordering the beheading of John the Baptist. Mark 6:26 tells us that because of those who *sat with him*, he did not want to refuse his stepdaughter's request. Herod was afraid to stand up for what was right—he feared his reputation and friendships more than he feared God. Paul wrote a strong exhortation to Timothy about the kind of people to stay away from (2 Timothy 3:1–5). Discuss this passage and the reasons you must be careful.

Peter's fear of men caused him to deny his *true* friend, Jesus, in Luke 22:54–60. Peter was more concerned with his reputation than with sticking up for and standing by Jesus. Standing by a friend in an unjust situation, regardless of what others think of you, builds character and will strengthen both you and your friend.

And get this! Your ability to choose good friends will also help you choose a good wife someday. This is important. There was a man who went down in history for his terrible choice of a companion: his wife. The Lord's opinion of Ahab, the king of Israel, is clear from 1 Kings 21:25: "There was never a man like Ahab, who sold himself to do evil in the eyes of the LORD, urged on by Jezebel his wife." Ahab clearly knew what was right. He had seen that the prophets of Baal were powerless, that Baal worship was a sham and heard all of Israel proclaim together, "The LORD—he is God!" (1 Kings 18:39). Ahab had witnessed God's power displayed through His messenger Elijah to hold back rain for three entire years, or to pour out torrents of water at a moment's notice. He followed God's prophet's directions to win battles against the mighty Aramean (Syrian) army. Yet *he passively watched* while his wife killed the Lord's prophets and fed the prophets of Baal at the king's table. He allowed her to seek the death of Elijah, despite the fact that Ahab himself was present at Mt. Carmel and did not disagree with Elijah's actions against the prophets of Baal. He participated in the death of Naboth, a righteous, innocent man, because of his selfishness and his wife's power-hungry wickedness. He built an altar to Baal and a temple of Baal in Samaria. God condemns the life of Ahab in no uncertain terms because he knew to do what was right but *was spurred on to evil by a poor choice of companion.*

Don't allow yourself to be double-minded, passive or weak in choosing your friends. Bad company corrupts morals (1 Corinthians 15:33).

Notes

Your ability to stand alone depends upon your willingness to be different and separate from the world.

Standing Alone

"'You are to be holy to me because I, the LORD, am holy, and I have set you apart from the nations to be my own.'"
Leviticus 20:26

"Gotta have it." "Be like Mike." "Can't live without it." You hear these catch phrases, or others like them, almost daily. The message of the world is that you need to fit in. Advertisers are constantly telling you that you will be popular in this world *if* you dress a particular way, own specific things and act in a certain manner. The message is that you can't be happy unless you are like everyone else. The implication is that we are all created to be just like each other.

When God was preparing the Israelites to go into the promised land of Canaan, He knew He was sending them into a sin-filled land that would tempt them and possibly distract them from their purpose. Many times God reminded these people that they belonged to Him and that their greatest happiness and satisfaction would come from holiness. Being holy meant that they would be *different* from the people around them. God's plan was for Israel to be a witness, an example and a light that pointed the other nations to the goodness and greatness of Him. By watching Israel, other nations should have been blessed and have wanted Israel's true God as their God.

The above verse is a powerful reminder that God's special purpose for you as His child is that you be holy and separate from the world and its ways. Holiness is about living rightly according to God's ways rather than the world's ways. It takes courage to be different from others and determination to stay on the right path. Don't confuse holiness with those who, in pride, act "holier than thou." Holiness is also not about a bunch of rules. Holiness is what brings happiness into your life, because when you live as God designed you to live, you will truly be happy. In addition to being happy personally, you will be a light and example to others.

The book *Jesus Freaks* tells stories of people throughout history who stood alone in the world and died for their faith in Jesus Christ. As martyrs, they died because they refused to give in to the world's pressure to deny Jesus when most people around them were willing to turn away from Him. The authors of this book say that "while we may not be called to martyr our lives . . . we must put selfish ways to death and march to a different beat. Then the world will see Jesus."[1] The authors also state that this often means a believer will have to "walk alone" in this life because his values are so different from the values of the world. This is the exhortation Paul gives in Romans 12:2, to not live according to the patterns of this world.

Micaiah's story in 1 Kings 22 and 2 Chronicles 18 is one of the greatest examples of standing for God's truth no matter what the cost. He was a prophet, a messenger from God who literally "stood alone" against 400 other false prophets. King Ahab never liked Micaiah because he said Micaiah never spoke good about him. The real issue was that Ahab didn't want to hear truth and obey God. Micaiah would not back down from the pressure and threat of so many against him. As Ahab's messenger brought Micaiah out, he even tried to prompt Micaiah by telling him to go along with what the other "prophets" had already said. Micaiah made a bold statement that should be the intent of every Christian—"I can tell him only what the LORD tells me" (1 Kings 22:14). There would be no compromise of truth on Micaiah's part. Micaiah is never heard from again after this incident. He was sent to prison for standing up and speaking God's truth. Though standing alone cost Micaiah greatly, he lived with something highly valuable and rare—a clean conscience. We also can be sure he was well rewarded in heaven for his commitment to God and determination to speak only the truth that God had revealed to him. His example is one for all Christians to follow.

Standing up and standing alone is something you will have to do even among your Christian friends at times. Micaiah's peers—fellow prophets—really should have had the same message from God as Micaiah. Instead, they appear to have been so eager to fit in and say what would please the king that they didn't speak truth. You may find yourself in a similar situation once in a while. You may be tempted to go along with what your Christian friends are all doing even when you know in your heart it isn't right for you. Remember, each Christian is growing at a different pace. Your friends' walk with God is individual and gradual—just as yours is—and each one struggles with different weaknesses and sins. This means that you must make many daily decisions based on what you know in your heart—and what the Bible says—is right, rather than by looking to your friends and going along with every suggestion you hear.

Standing up and standing alone is something you will have to do even among your Christian friends at times.

Sometimes you will be hesitant to go along with your friends because you are unsure whether what they are doing is right. You'll need to talk over your choices with God in your heart, and if you aren't certain, it's usually best to wait and hold back. You may be the only one in a crowd willing to say you aren't comfortable with a certain activity, movie or behavior. If you are unable

to convince a friend or a group about it, you will have to stand by yourself and let them go. This is good practice, though, and it won't be the last time it is necessary.

Paul warned about being part of questionable behaviors. In 2 Thessalonians 3:6, he instructed believers to "withdraw from every *brother* who walks disorderly"(NKJV). He was speaking of disorderly Christians in this passage. These guys were careless and negligent in their daily work and behavior, and Paul told his readers to walk away from them. This Bible passage is telling you to be wise, discerning and observant of the Christians you hang out with. Some can be bad influences. Hanging with a "disorderly brother" is like being a companion of fools (remember Proverbs 13:20 from the last chapter?). When you find yourself in a situation where a Christian acquaintance or friend is making a bad choice, be strong, speak out, and walk away if necessary.

"The wicked man flees though no one pursues, but the righteous are as bold as a lion" (Proverbs 28:1).

Your personal success in standing alone depends upon your willingness to be different and separate from the world. A willingness to stand alone begins in your heart and requires a commitment of the heart. Daniel made a committed decision long before he would have to stand alone for rightness. Daniel 1:8 says that he "resolved not to *defile* himself" with all the worldly pleasures available to him in the king's court. When something is defiled, it is changed in a way that makes it less than the best that it should be. That means it is polluted, contaminated or corrupted. Daniel wanted to be the very best physically and spiritually. He knew that there were many pleasurable things in the king's court. Daniel also knew that these foods and activities might pollute his body and make it less than the best for God. Daniel had guts and courage. He was a "man's man," a brave guy who was willing to stand up to anyone, against any odds to do what he knew was right. This is because he knew he had God with him, by his side. His commitment to be separate and holy at a young age strengthened Daniel for more difficult situations, such as the dooming message written by a hand on the wall in Daniel 5. This commitment prepared Daniel for each instance in the future when he would need to take a stand for God when everyone else was participating in what was offensive to God.

Review Daniel 6, where King Darius decreed that no one could pray to any god except him. Daniel would not compromise his faith because he had made a commitment to holiness. Notice that this commitment was made *before* the situation came up. Verse 4 says that his enemies could find no fault or error in Daniel because he was faithful. This is because Daniel had been practicing living for God. His daily practice of holy living in private times prepared Daniel to stand alone publicly (in front of people) in this big test. Each chapter of the Book of Daniel shows Daniel's continued boldness as well as the increased risks he took. Kings came and went, and empires rose and fell throughout his lifetime, but Daniel was always willing to stand alone as he stood up for what was right. What a great example! Daniel stood up to captains of the king's guard, to other wise men and governors, and to kings themselves in good times and bad. No matter what the situation, the location or the ruler of the nation, Daniel was ready to stand alone for God.

Will you make a commitment in your heart to stand alone even when people might give you a hard time? Do your friends want to follow your God because they see you boldly and energetically sold out to Him?

Will you make a commitment in your heart to stand alone even when people might give you a hard time?

Situations are much more tempting when you haven't made a commitment *ahead of time* to do what is right. Wavering in indecision causes you to be more likely to give in to what is wrong or what is not the best for your life. Preparing yourself ahead of time by making a commitment to holiness will help you stay determined to live undefiled. Think about the habit you have of brushing your teeth every day. Do you stand in front of the mirror and debate the value and health benefits of brushing your teeth every day? Or do you just do it because you know it's the right thing to do? Most likely you decided long ago that brushing your teeth was going to be a regular part of your life. This means you don't have to go through a daily debate over whether or not you need to brush your teeth. This decision made ahead of time saves you the mental agony of running a daily, situation-by-situation debate.

The example of brushing teeth is very simple, but it illustrates well the concept that decisions for godliness made in your mind and heart *ahead of time* keep you from wavering when a situation of possible compromise comes your way. There are many decisions for godliness that are necessary for your good spiritual health, just like brushing teeth is necessary for your good physical health. Take time to think about decisions you can make now that will protect you from wavering in the future. Will you prepare yourself for the times when you will need to stand alone for rightness by practicing holy and faithful living now?

When you understand that God has a specific plan for your life and that He has given you gifts to use for Him to bless other people, then you will be better able to stand alone and apart from this world. You need not have an appetite for the temporary stuff of this world, nor feel a strong need to fit in with everyone else. The closer you get to the Lord, the more *out of place* you will feel in this world because this world is not your real home. The Bible says that you are a stranger in this world, preparing for the day when you get to live with Jesus in heaven (Philippians 3:20). This means you will stand out and be different from others as you stand up for righteousness and demonstrate godliness.

Standing up for what is right causes you to *stand out* in a world that is full of wrongdoing. As you are honest with people, you stand out as one who is trustworthy; as you encourage and build up others, you stand out because the world is competitive and cuts others down. Be glad that you are known for taking a strong stand rather than following a crowd. It has been said, "He who stands for nothing will fall for anything." If you don't have confidence in your heart about what is right, you are in danger of falling for any idea or trend that comes your way and are in danger of falling into sin.

"'Come out from them and be separate,' says the Lord" (2 Corinthians 6:17).

Don't Forget It 🖙 *(answers on page 121)*

1. Holiness is _____ _____ according to God's ways rather than the world's ways.

2. Living in holiness causes me to be an _____ to others.

3. Strong convictions about what is right will keep me from _____ for anything.

4. Standing up for what is right means I will _____ _____ from the world.

Further Study 📖

Specific passages declare that God has given different gifts to each individual. Romans 12:4–8 says that you are a part of the Body of Christ and you have an individual role to play in it. While the world is telling you that you aren't worth much unless you are like everyone else, God is telling you that *your value is in being different from others*. What is it you like doing right now? Have you prayed and asked God how He might develop what you enjoy doing now so that you can use that gift to serve Him? You will be wise to begin praying as a young man that God will show you what your gifts are and how you might be able to use them in the future. This vision for your future will give you the desire to stay close to God and live your life for Him now, rather than trying hard to fit in with what is popular or trendy.

God gave you individuality. If He wanted everyone to "be like Mike," He would have created cookie-cutter people on the earth. How boring that would be!

Study 2 Corinthians 6:17–7:1. This is God's call to come apart from the world and cleanse yourself from its filthiness. Discuss what can "defile" you and cause you to stumble when you need to make a stand.

Study Acts 4:13–31 and 5:22–32, making note of the priority Peter, John and the apostles had. "Enable your servants to speak your word with great boldness" (4:29) and "We must obey God rather than men" (5:29) are worthy prayers of commitment to standing alone in this world.

Look through Ephesians 4:11–16, 1 Corinthians 12:27–31 and 1 Corinthians 14:26, and pray about gifts that God is developing in you. Read through 1 Corinthians 13 and ask above all that He give you the gift of love for people as you stand up for truth.

Notes ✐

_____

_____

_____

_____

_____

_____

_____

_____

_____

_____

[1] d.c. Talk. *Jesus Freaks* (Tulsa, Okla.: Albury Publishing, 1999), p. 8.

Every decision you make is based on knowledge, no matter how much or how little you have.

Knowledge

"That you may live a life worthy of the Lord and may please him in every way: bearing fruit in every good work, growing in the knowledge of God."
Colossians 1:10

"'My people are destroyed for lack of knowledge.'"
Hosea 4:6

So you want to buy a new skateboard? How will you choose the best one? No doubt you'll march into a local store and buy the coolest-looking one, right? By now you've probably learned that the shiniest and brightest things are not always the best quality. In reality, you would probably read up on the different kinds of skateboards and the advantages and cost of each one. You would probably talk with people you know who are good skateboarders to find out which ones have worked best for them. You might also go to several stores and talk with experts about skateboards before you actually bought the one that would be right for you. Why? Because you want to maximize your benefits and minimize your regrets. You want a skateboard that will get you the best for your money. You want to make an investment that will go the long haul, giving you the best performance and smoothest ride. In this process, you gather knowledge first and then apply it to your situation before acting on it and spending your money. Good decisions are usually best made by gathering accurate information and using it.

Knowledge plays a very important part in your Christian life too. Every decision you make is based on knowledge, no matter how much or how little you have. Decisions that seem really important to you should cause you to dig for more information that will help you make the best and right decisions. That knowledge, however, is only helpful if you put it to use. *Knowing* what is right and *doing* it are different matters. This is where wisdom comes in. There is a difference between being smart and being wise. Smart people might be full of all kinds of knowledge, but they can also make very foolish decisions. Gathering facts and learning principles is important and useful, but only if you will *use* them to make good choices. Solomon had a great amount of knowledge, but he rejected its wisdom and lived his life for his own pleasure. His knowledge caused him to be proud.

Wisdom, on the other hand, brings humility. Wisdom understands that there is more that you *don't* know than you do know. How incredibly deep and rich is the wisdom and knowledge of God! No man will ever learn *all* there is to know about life and living wisely (Romans 11:33–36).

Read the story of Jeroboam in 1 Kings 12:25–33. Unfortunately, as a leader, Solomon's rejection of the knowledge of God caused Israel to follow in his path. God was grieved over the way Solomon had turned his people away from Him. In 1 Kings 11:31, God declared that He would divide the kingdom of Israel and give ten of the twelve tribes to Jeroboam. It was God's desire to have this new leader, Jeroboam, lead Israel back to Him. Instead, Jeroboam built two golden calves for his people to worship because he was afraid that if they traveled down to the temple in Jerusalem, they would desert him as king. Notice how Jeroboam introduced these new gods to Israel. "Here are your gods, O Israel, who brought you up out of Egypt" (v. 28).

What's wrong with this statement? Why didn't it strike the people as being wrong and out of place? These were the exact words of Aaron when he presented Israel with a similar golden calf centuries before. This should have been obvious to the Israelites, but instead, they *lacked knowledge* of their past and God's goodness to their ancestors (part of the fallout of Solomon's poor leadership). Had they *known* God and been students of their faith, they would have never accepted these useless idols.

Their acceptance of the calves tells us these people didn't have a loving relationship with God and no longer had knowledge of Him that they applied to their daily lives. About 500 years had passed since the event with Aaron, but apparently there was still a trace of knowledge for Jeroboam to have referred to the "gods" who brought them out of Egypt. Sadly, Jeroboam set a bad trend by leading Israel further away from God, and there was never a good king in northern Israel after him.

America has been in existence for a little more than 200 years and is following the same path—forgetting God, having little or no knowledge of Him and His ways. Psalm 119:11 says, "I have hidden your word in my heart that I might not sin against you." Knowledge of God and His ways can keep a Christian from sin. The saying is true: "Either this book (the Bible) will keep you from sin, or sin will keep you from this book."

Knowledge of God and His ways can keep a Christian from sin.

The world is at new levels of sophistication with incredible computer technology and powerful electronic gadgets. A person could easily think that the world has arrived at its greatest level of accomplishments. Unfortunately, with all this technology and intelligence, God has been left out. Knowledge of God and of His heart's desire for His children is at an all-time low, much like it was in Jeroboam's day.

For hundreds of years God sent warnings to Israel and patiently waited for His people to turn back to Him. Finally, God sent a message to Israel through the prophet Hosea. The message was that their enemies, the Babylonians, would carry them into captivity because His people had for-

gotten Him and had rejected knowledge of Him. Second Timothy 3:7 says that in the last days people will be lovers of themselves, always learning and never able to come to the knowledge of the truth. This is because they reject God as the Giver of truth. Once again history is repeating itself.

God's Word is the knowledge for all of life and provides direction that is clear and useful for each day. By consulting His Word, the Bible, and praying for direction, you are developing an active relationship with God and learning to respond to His Spirit in you. Individuals who grew up knowing God will tell you that the verses they learned in their youth are the ones that have come back to their memory at needed times as adults. Jesus said that this is the work of the Holy Spirit. He told His disciples in John 14:26 that the Holy Spirit would bring back to their memory what He had taught them. The disciples had spent three years with Jesus, learning from His life and His teachings. When Jesus went back up to heaven, God's Holy Spirit used the knowledge they had gained from being with Jesus as *practical* understanding for their lives. Knowledge and understanding go together.

Colossians 1:10, which is printed at the beginning of this chapter, tells you to increase in your knowledge of God. Proverbs 9:10 says, "The fear of the LORD is the beginning of wisdom." This means that respecting and honoring God is the start of gaining knowledge. It is important to balance your school studies with an effort to increase your knowledge of God through the Bible. This will help you balance your life and keep God in focus as the source of all intelligence. Growing in your knowledge of God will give you direction for your life and the ability to tell right from wrong. Become a student of the Word! It will be a light for your path in a dark world (Psalm 119:105).

It is very important to be a good student, to learn all you can and sharpen your mind so that you can have many choices of career and service for the Lord when you are older. God has given you a good mind and He expects you to use it responsibly as you are growing up. Remember, Jesus said that the greatest commandment is to love God with all your heart, with all your soul and *with all your mind* (Matthew 22:37). God wants you to study and learn all you can about the world in which you live because it points to Him as the source of all creativity and wisdom. As people become more knowledgeable, they often begin to worship what was created or their intelligence rather than God. They begin to think that their discoveries and accomplishments come from within themselves rather than give credit to God and thank Him for their sharp mind.

Colossians 2:3 says that *all* the treasures of wisdom and knowledge are found in Jesus. Wisdom for life comes from knowing and gaining understanding of Jesus' words and His life. Second Timothy 2:15 states the mission well: "Do your best to present yourself to God as one approved, a workman who does not need to be ashamed and who correctly handles the word of truth." You will be the leader of your home someday, a teacher of the Word to your children. If you dig in now and learn all you can about the Lord, you will be more confident and secure about your place in the world. You also will be better prepared to be a leader in the future, and you will be ready to spend eternity with Jesus.

"Gold there is, and rubies in abundance, but lips that speak knowledge are a rare jewel" (Proverbs 20:15).

Don't Forget It 👉 *(answers on page 121)*

1. Knowledge is only useful to me if I _____ it and apply it to my life.

2. One benefit of increasing my knowledge of God is that it helps keep me from _____.

3. God's _____ _____ brings truth I have learned back to my mind when I need it.

Further Study 📖

Daniel 1:17 says that God gave the gift of knowledge to Daniel and three other men, Hananiah, Mishael and Azariah (can you remember their other, more well known names?). These guys were recognized for their ability to learn and work hard and were brought in among Babylon's "wise men." Though Daniel and his friends were in a foreign land, in enemy territory, they worked hard in their studies and the king found them to be *ten times* smarter than all his wisest men (v. 20)!

Though they were studying Babylonian culture (representative of secular knowledge), they remained focused on God, recognizing Him as the source of all knowledge. Whether they studied astrology, philosophy, literature or other sciences (vv. 5, 17), Daniel and his friends incorporated God into all of their life. The knowledge they gained only increased their reverence and awe of the Creator of the universe. Daniel even gave God the credit for his knowledge when placed before the king (Daniel 2:27–28). As believers in God, the studious efforts of these men caused them to be teachers and leaders over Babylon's own wise men, who didn't know God. Daniel and his friends had great opportunity to point fellow students to God even as they made new discoveries.

Many Bible scholars believe that it was the influence of Daniel and his friends that caused the wise men from the East to come in search of the baby Jesus many years later. They believe that Daniel put together prophecies about the Messiah and taught the astrologers to look for an unusual star that would announce the coming of a great king of the Jews. This teaching would have been passed on through the generations of Babylon's wise men. The result of these studies was a blessing of wealth (gold, frankincense and myrrh) for Mary and Joseph, which they needed during their years in Egypt. In other words, all this scientific study was done with Jesus, the Messiah, as the focus, just as your knowledge should be balanced and focused on Him.

God has a purpose for the teachings you are receiving, including school (secular knowledge), church, family devotions and your personal study of the Bible. Learn all you can, keeping God in focus as you learn, and watch and see how He will use that knowledge to bless the people around you!

"This is what the LORD says:
'Let not the wise man boast of his wisdom
or the strong man boast of his strength
or the rich man boast of his riches,
but let him who boasts boast about this:
that he understands and knows me,
that I am the LORD, who exercises kindness,
justice and righteousness on earth,
for in these I delight.'" (Jeremiah 9:23–24)

Other passages on the value of knowledge and its link to wisdom include Psalm 119:66, Proverbs 1:22–2:7, 8:9–11, 9:10 and 24:5, Ecclesiastes 7:12, Isaiah 33:6, Jeremiah 4:22, Daniel 2:21 and Romans 15:4.

Read 2 Timothy 3:16–17 and 1 Peter 3:15, and discuss the results of good knowledge of the Word: knowing how to answer others and being complete and equipped for service.

Notes

Set an example for others in speech, in life, in love, in faith and in purity ... this is the ultimate cool image.

Image

"Don't let anyone look down on you because you are young, but set an example for the believers in speech, in life, in love, in faith and in purity."
1 Timothy 4:12

Every guy wants an "image," a way of declaring his individuality and special character. He wants to look cool, talk cool and be cool. He wants to be noticed as a unique, special person, and he wants to be appreciated for his traits. Paul told Timothy how to create that special image while he was still young. Paul described five categories that make up the right image as an example to the world that you are a believer in and follower of Jesus. This is the ultimate "cool image" that stands out in a world that has few models to follow. Paul's instruction to Timothy was to put these qualities into his life while he was still young so that those around him would have a godly example to follow. The categories listed in the verse above come together and create an image, or representation of a person. The order of this list is significant. Take a closer look at each quality. (Note: You may want to take a separate day to study each category.)

Paul described five categories that make up the right image as an example to the world that you are a believer in and follower of Jesus.

Speech

Speech is listed first for a good reason—the way a person talks says a lot about him. You might see someone from a distance and think you want him to be your friend by the way he looks, but overhearing him talk to someone else may show you otherwise. The words that come out of your mouth reveal what's inside your heart. Jesus explained this in Matthew 15:11–19. Your speech says a lot to people about what you are like on the inside. James said it is not right that both blessing and cursing should come out of the same mouth (James 3:10). The words you say have the ability to bless others or hurt them. Remember, it's your choice as to which kind of words you speak, but once said, you can't take them back.

This is most challenging with those closest to you—your family. It's not easy to respond decently when your brother or sister is bugging you. This is where you need to practice speaking *graciously*. This is also important when you feel someone has wrongly assumed you did something, or you have been asked to do a job you feel is unfair. Sometimes saying nothing says more than words can express. Pray that God would keep your heart pure so that you might speak words that show respect to others.

"A wise man's heart guides his mouth, and his lips promote instruction. Pleasant words are a honeycomb, sweet to the soul and healing to the bones" (Proverbs 16:23–24).

Doctors say that your hearing determines much of your speech. That is logical since children growing up in Germany speak German and children living in France speak French, and so on. These children speak what they hear. The next conclusion from this medical understanding is that children with hearing problems have difficulty speaking clearly. This is because *what a person hears teaches him how to speak*. This demonstrates a powerful spiritual point. What you are listening to will determine how you speak. Are you hearing healthy conversation that influences your ability to speak well of others and encourage them? Or do your friends talk negatively about everything? If they do, watch out. You may quickly find yourself speaking like they do. Proof of this principle is seen in the many trendy phrases and expressions that get passed around. They naturally become part of your vocabulary because you are *hearing* them.

This principle is incredibly important when you consider all that you listen to on TV, in movies and on your CD player. What is the conversation like in the movies or TV shows you watch? What are the lyrics of your music doing to your speech? Are the words you hear full of life and happiness, or are they negative, biting and full of sarcasm and ridicule? You need to understand that what you hear greatly affects how you speak. This may mean that you need to change or adjust what you hear.

The words you speak have a great effect on your life. The Bible notes that the tongue is small but has great power. James compares the tongue to a small rudder that determines the direction of a large ship, or a small bit in the mouth of a large, powerful horse (James 3:3–4). In the same way, your words can determine your direction or destination in life.

"The tongue has the power of life and death" (Proverbs 18:21).

Further Study on Speech

Look up the following passages and pray about areas in which you need help: Psalm 34:13 and 39:1, Proverbs 10:11, 19–20, 12:18–19 and 29:11, Ephesians 4:29, Colossians 4:6 and the classic passage on taming the tongue, James 3:2–12.

Note to Parents: How do you and your children *hear* God? Do you read the Bible and hear God's love, tenderness and grace, or do you hear constant judgment, wrath and anger? The way you hear the messages of God affects how you speak of Him to your family and others. The Old Testament is full of God's patience and mercy towards His people. The many warnings in the Bible should be heard as God wanting His best for your life. It is important that you and your children hear God's Word correctly: conviction is from the Holy Spirit; condemnation is from Satan.

Life

Life is about the way you walk. Some people are all talk and no action. Others are all talk but their actions contradict their talk. Colossians 4:5 says to walk wisely in this life because "outsiders," non-Christians, are watching. Your walk and talk need to go together with consistency, like teamwork. You've probably heard the saying, "Actions speak louder than words." If you identify yourself as a Christian, it is important that you also walk as God would have one of His children walk.

Saint Francis of Assisi said that every believer should be a constant witness and use words only when necessary. His point is that your life, your actions (the way you treat people), are to be a reflection of Jesus. He is the image you want to portray through your conduct. Saint Francis lived a very simple life; he was very generous towards everyone who crossed his path while not being attached to material possessions himself. He gave of his time and energy, giving advice and direction to people as well as living by that counsel himself. Years later, communist leader Vladimir Lenin said that if there had been ten of

Saint Francis, there would have been no need for a revolution. Lenin was saying that if only ten people had lived as Saint Francis of Assisi had, the people in his country would not have felt so desperate, but rather would have been provided for in every way. Saint Francis of Assisi lived a life that spoke a clear message and impacted all those around him.

"Even a child is known by his actions, by whether his conduct is pure and right" (Proverbs 20:11).

"Do not merely listen to the word, and so deceive yourselves. Do what it says" (James 1:22).

Further Study on Life

Consider the following passages, which speak of the importance of your life-walk: Ephesians 4:1–3 and 5:15–17, Philippians 1:27, Colossians 1:10 and 1 Thessalonians 2:12.

Love

Can you imagine a love that won't die? One man in history actually possessed such a love. No one could kill him because his love for God's people couldn't be killed. Tradition says that it was impossible for the Roman emperor to kill the apostle John because his love wouldn't die. John was known as the apostle of love, not just because he wrote about it, but also because he *lived* a life of demonstrating God's love to people. Wanting to give him a disgraceful death, the emperor decided to throw John into a vat of boiling oil. John prayed as he was being let down into the oil and continued to pray, only louder, while in the oil. Disgusted that the watching crowd grew wild with excitement, the emperor ordered John to be removed from his sight. John's supernatural love for God couldn't be burned out.

Jesus said that the true mark of His disciples would be their love for one another (John 13:35). The main characteristic of followers of Jesus is to be the love they show for one another. That's a sobering thought, isn't it? It's been said that if those who call themselves Christians were truly demonstrating love, there would be no need for government help with feeding and clothing the poor. All would be taken care of because of the giving love of the Christians in this world.

Some people are hard to love. Sometimes it is difficult to show love when you've been hurt. Sometimes you just don't want to show love and kindness to people because you don't *feel* like doing it. But, "whoever loves his brother lives in the light, and there is nothing in him to make him stumble" (1 John 2:10). Getting past your negative feelings about a situation or person and showing love is a great sign of growth in you. It's also an awesome example to others around you and can help show them Jesus. Kindness and love are the marks that make you different from those who belittle and put down their brothers and sisters, their parents or even their friends.

The Bible says that if someone claims he loves God but hates his brother, he is a liar (1 John 4:20). Your family should be the first to receive your love. Why does it sometimes seem easier to show love to friends than to family? Because when you live with your family, you see the faults of each member more clearly and more often than you see the faults of your friends. This means you have to *choose* to overlook these faults and be kind. Love is not something you can create. When it is hard to love those closest to you, you need to ask God to fill you with His love. Love is a gift from God. He is the source of love and the One who fills your heart with love so you can share it with others.

"And now these three remain: faith, hope and love. But the greatest of these is love" (1 Corinthians 13:13).

Further Study on Love

Read the short book of 1 John, highlighting the specific verses on love, the source of love and what John says about those who lack God's love. Pray that God would fill you with genuine love for the people He has brought into your life.

First Peter 4:8 says that love covers a multitude of sins. (Look also at Proverbs 17:9.) Psalm 32:1–2 says that the man whose sin is forgiven will be blessed, or happy. Discuss the importance of appreciating and enjoying forgiveness of sin from God and the need to forgive and overlook the sins of others, as Colossians 3:13–14 instructs.

Faith

"Look at those muscles! These guys are huge! There's no way we'll ever win!" Twelve people were looking at the same situation. Ten said there was no way they could win; two said there was no way they could lose. It all depends on your view of life and to whom or what you are comparing your situation. Is the glass in your life half empty or half full? This old question about your view of life challenges you to look at what good you have going for you, not what seems to be missing. Two spies decided their glass was half full. Giants are enormous compared with men, but giants are puny compared with God. These guys walked by faith and not by sight (2 Corinthians 5:7). "We should go up and take possession of the land, for we can certainly do it," Caleb and

Joshua said (Numbers 13:30). They were not trusting in their own muscle power. They simply believed the promise of God that He had given the land of Canaan to them. They were trusting in God's strength, not their own.

Read Joshua and Caleb's story in Numbers 13 and notice their response to God's instructions. They understood that God was bigger than the giants in Canaan, and they had faith in God's ability to enable them to do what He had told them to do (Numbers 13:30, 14:7–10). Sometimes there will be "giant" problems in your life, but 1 John 4:4 says that the One who is in you is greater than your enemy in the world. God's power is not blocked by any giant.

Your "walk" on this earth is also to be marked by your faith in Jesus and loyalty to all that He stands for. As you walk with God, others will see your trust in God's way of working in your life. Hebrews 11:1 says that faith is being certain about what you do not see. When you look out a window and see a tree being bent by the wind, you are certain it is windy. You see the *effect* of the wind even though it is impossible to see the wind. This is like your faith in God. You don't see Him physically, but you see the effect, or difference, He makes in your life. You put your trust in Jesus *by faith*, with absolute conviction He is the only way to heaven. You pray to God *by faith*, believing and knowing that He hears, He has the power to act and that He will do what is best for your life. You see the effect of God answering your prayers. You obey His word *by faith*, believing that His ways are right and will keep you from falling into sin. You trust and hope in the goodness of God *by faith*, expecting the very best from Him. In reading the Bible, you see the effect of God in the lives of real people and you know that He is real, even though you cannot see Him. Let your faith become the mark for which you are known.

"Now faith is being sure of what we hope for and certain of what we do not see. . . . And without faith it is impossible to please God, because anyone who comes to him must believe that he exists and that he rewards those who earnestly seek him" (Hebrews 11:1, 6).

"'You will seek me and find me when you seek me with all your heart'" (Jeremiah 29:13).

Further Study on Faith

The Arameans (also known as Syrians) had been raiding Israel and threatening war (2 Kings 6:8–23). Elisha's servant went outside one morning and panicked. Their city of Dothan was surrounded by the Aramean army. Elisha, however, was calm. His perspective was an example of great faith. "Those who are with us are more than those who are with them," Elisha told his servant (v. 16). Elisha's faith is a model for the difficult situations you face. Saint Augustine said, "Faith is to believe what we do not see, and the reward of this faith is to see what we believe." Elisha's faith was rewarded in seeing what he believed in—that God and His heavenly host were with him. If God is for you, who can be against you? (Romans 8:31). Praying the promises of the Bible is a great way to develop your faith. Remember, nothing is too hard for the Lord (Jeremiah 32:17).

Make this song, "Eyes of Faith," your prayer when you lack faith or are afraid:

Give me eyes to see the invisible
Give me ears to hear Your voice
Give me faith to believe the impossible
And strength to make the choice
To follow You when I can go no further
To hear Your voice and quietly obey
To go on when others only murmur
To stand steadfast in Your ways
Father of faith, give me vision
Saviour of strength, keep me strong
Spirit of love, be my devotion
That I may carry on.

— Rick Vestnys

Purity

"Monkey see, monkey do." What you see greatly affects your behavior. The psalmist said that he would set nothing unclean before his eyes (Psalm 101:3). He understood something very important: what you *see* greatly influences your mind and your heart. Images that you see on the TV screen, in the movies, in magazines or on the computer stay with you a long time and flash back

in your memory. Jesus spoke very strongly about the power of the eye. In Matthew 6:22–23, He said that the eye is the lamp of the body. He said that if your eye is good, your whole body will be full of light, but if your eye is bad, *your whole body will be full of darkness.*

Satan is very aware of the power of what you see, and he wants to use it to pull you down. The Bible says he is a roaring lion, seeking someone to devour (1 Peter 5:8). Satan has devoured many people through visual imagery. Many young people and even more adults are hooked on the Internet because they started looking at pictures they shouldn't be seeing. Most of these people didn't understand the strong hold that images have and are now addicted. They didn't resist their curiosity, and by allowing their eyes to see counterfeits of God's design in physical beauty, their entire body is now full of darkness. Many people have become addicted to inappropriate pictures, videos or chat room conversations on the Internet and their families have been torn apart as a result. Here is another area where you see how God's Word fits every generation throughout history. Psalm 140:5 says, "Proud men have hidden a snare for me; they have spread out the cords of their *net* and have set traps for me along my path." The Inter*net* can be a trap and needs to be handled very carefully. Respect the advice of pastors and your parents on this, even if you don't yet understand it.

Remember that everywhere you go, you take Jesus with you. Is there real value to what you are watching, or is it just wasting valuable time? Does He want to be watching that TV show or movie, or would you be embarrassed to have Him sitting next to you? Your innocence and purity is evidence to your friends that you are a Christian. It is good when you do not understand talk about certain shows because you haven't seen them. Be thankful that your mind has not been polluted with those images. Ephesians 5:11–12 says that it is not right to even speak about the things done in secret by those who walk in darkness.

Jesus' instructions to the men He sent out was that they were to be *as wise as serpents and innocent or harmless as doves* (Matthew 10:16). Make this your life prayer as the days become more evil.

"Pure and undefiled religion before God and the Father is this: . . . to keep oneself unspotted from the world" (James 1:27, NKJV).

There you have it! Be an example to others in your *total body language*—the way you talk, the way you walk and what you allow yourself to be a part of.

Being a starter on the varsity basketball team as a high school freshman could have caused Brandon to become a target for the other guys. But the coach told his parents that he had earned their respect by his consistency. The coach shared a story of some comments made during practice. One of the guys swore about missing a shot. Another player corrected him, telling him not to speak like that in front of Brandon. Brandon had never put them down or said that he didn't appreciate their language; the guys just knew from his life that it wasn't appropriate in front of Brandon. A senior on the team responded, "I don't think Brandon has ever had a bad thought in his life." That statement said all that needed to be said about Brandon's example of godly speech, life, faith and purity. "Witness constantly; when necessary use words." By being a living example, the stage has been set for Brandon to back up his actions by sharing with his friends that Jesus has made this difference in his life.

Further Study on Purity

Romans 12:1–2 and Colossians 3:1–2 are verses worthy of memorizing. They remind you that your affections are not to be focused on worldly things. These verses give the answer for renewing your mind: continually being in the Word of God. The Bible speaks of reading the Word as a way of washing and cleansing you from the ungodliness of the world (Psalm 119:9 and Ephesians 5:26). After spending a day in the world, at school, you hear or see things that are contrary to godliness and purity. The remedy to this is being renewed and transformed from that thinking by the Word of God. This is why memorizing verses is necessary. This was Jesus' method of resisting temptation, or "renewing" His mind, in Matthew 4. You may not have a Bible with you at all times, but God's Spirit will remind you of verses you have memorized when you need help or assurance from Him.

First John 2:15–17 explains the source of impurity: the lust of the flesh (wanting to satisfy your own desires), the lust of the eyes (seeing things that pull your heart away from God) and the pride of life (thinking you can handle your life your own way). Solomon was one who seemed to think himself able to live apart from what God said was right. His lust and pride turned him away from God and caused the split of the nation of Israel. His life is a lesson that no one can be happy or satisfied with what the world has to offer (see 1 Kings 11).

Other verses to study include Psalm 9:15–16, Proverbs 4:23–27, Matthew 5:8, Philippians 4:8 and James 1:13–15.

Make the following verses your prayer of commitment to purity:

"I will set before my eyes no vile thing" (Psalm 101:3).

"Turn my eyes away from worthless things; preserve my life according to your word" (Psalm 119:37).

Don't Forget It ☞ *(answers on page 121)*

1. The words that I say have the potential to _____ others or _____ them.

2. What I _____ greatly affects how I speak.

3. My walk and my talk need to be _____ with each other.

4. As a Christian, I should be known by my _____ for people.

5. My _____ should be the first to receive my love.

6. _____ is being certain of what I do not see, just as I am certain that the wind blows.

7. The images I see in movies or magazines will come _____ to me.

8. If my eye is bad, my whole body will be full of _____ (Matthew 6:22–23).

Notes

The best leaders work alongside
and encourage those they direct.

Leadership

*"When he (Jesus) saw the crowds, he had compassion on them,
because they were harassed and helpless, like sheep without a shepherd."*
Matthew 9:36

"'Whoever wants to become great among you must be your servant.'"
Matthew 20:26

Let's say you have started a new job taking orders for a catalog business. You have no experience in this work, but the boss is willing to train you. You arrive on your first day, eager and ready to learn. Your boss is extremely busy that particular day and tells you that he doesn't have the time he thought he would to walk you through the procedures. He gives you a handbook and tells you to read through it to learn how to input the data and record orders. Very soon, the phone lines are busy and he tells you, "You're on. Pick up the phone and start right in." You'd be frustrated, right? Why? Because you would feel pushed into the job, without adequate training; and even if you could have learned it all from a manual, no one would be available to answer your questions.

The best way to learn a new skill or job is to have someone walk you through it. You need someone to follow, someone to help you through the rough spots and give you advice. Success in a business depends on good leadership. Leaders have to be available to the workers, but *the best leaders work alongside and encourage those they direct*. Many businesses have discovered the principle of "leading by example" with respect to a position or a specific project or job. This has been proven true many times, especially in the military. There have been times when countries lost battles because the leaders gave orders to their men and then stayed behind and let the least-trained men lead the troops into the conflict. This caused the troops to be less certain of their duties, less loyal and less willing to risk their lives for their countries. The United States military trains its leaders to serve and work alongside the men and women, leading by example.

The world today is lacking good leaders.

The world today is lacking good leaders. Many people have the mistaken idea that leaders get to sit back in a chair, give orders and watch everyone else do the work. There is also an error in thinking that there are exceptions to the standard rules for leaders. Does this kind of leadership appeal to you? Would you like to make demands of employees but behave differently yourself? It would be like your Mom setting a plate of vegetables in front of you, explaining how valuable and nutritional they are, while setting a bowl of ice cream down for herself.

Solid leaders are those who have a strong commitment to good character. They hold *themselves* accountable for proper attitudes, integrity and honesty. Jesus would look at modern society with the same compassion as He did in Matthew 9:36 (see verse on previous page). The Bible uses the picture of a shepherd as a leader because of the way a shepherd cares for the sheep. A good shepherd puts aside his own comfort and does whatever is necessary to take care of the sheep: leading them to the best grazing land and fresh water, sleeping in front of the gate of the pen at night in order to protect them from predators, and going to great lengths to rescue one that has wandered away. In other words, the shepherd-leader is a servant to the sheep. This is true leadership in God's eyes. Too many of the world's leaders today are in the role for personal gain: fame, money, reputation and power. These motives cause men to

compromise and fall into sin all too often. Jesus models the best method of leadership.

The Bible teaches that, by God's design, you will have a role of leadership in your own home when you grow up. Good leadership is learned through serving. This is because serving others teaches you to think of their needs. It teaches you to think of what's best for everyone, not just for yourself. Putting aside your personal desires and placing the desires of others first is challenging. That is where a true leader stands out. You will need this skill as the head of your family someday (and very likely in your job).

Ephesians 5:22–33 gives instructions for men as leaders of their home. Specifically, good leadership is shown through love and service. Serving is the outward demonstration of the love of God that is in you. This means you will have to continually ask God to fill you with His love for others. Decisions you make for your family require that you take into consideration the needs and desires of each family member. This often will cause you to sacrifice your personal desire for the good of the whole family. You must have a willingness to "lay down your life" for them (John 10:15). At other times you will need to be strong enough to stand up for what is right and obey what God is telling you to do. Men who want control and power over their wives and children do not make good leaders. But men who graciously serve their families and direct them in the Word of God are respected and loved. If you have godly love for the people around you, you will have what is needed for leadership.

This principle is also true for you as you are growing up. Good leaders don't boss people around on the football field or hand out orders on the school project while doing nothing themselves. Good leaders are willing to do the work necessary for the successful completion of a goal, setting the standard for others around them to follow.

No one becomes a leader overnight. These young years are for you to practice good decision-making and leadership skills. These years are preparing you for the future roles you will have as the leader of your family and/or possibly as head of a business. Daily situations provide opportunities for you to build leadership skills into your life—group projects in school, sports teams, music groups or worship teams. There may also be places in your church for you to show leadership, such as helping in a classroom of younger children. If you have younger brothers or sisters, you have an opportunity to practice leadership by example at home. In all these situations, you will discover that good leadership requires work.

Read Mark 10:35–45 and notice the effect of James' and John's desire to have a position above the other disciples. Verse 41 says the other ten disciples were "indignant" with James and John, who desired to become "favored." No doubt you have seen this in school, where someone wants to be noticed as better than the others. True leaders work heartily and serve loyally in whatever role they have, and if that labor leads to higher positions, they continue to focus on serving God in that role. Leadership outside of your home, in the church or on the job is not to be desired just so others will notice you. Being chosen the captain of your soccer team, for instance, is an opportunity for you to be an example of a hard worker and to encourage the other team members to do their best. It is not an opportunity for you to be the boss.

Leadership is to be desired as an avenue to serve God in a way that will bless others and make a difference in your world. God's style of leadership is others-centered, meaning that you work at making life better for other people. Right now, as a young man, you have the opportunity to practice true leadership by your example in your home, school and extracurricular activities. It may not seem cool to serve others, but it develops the right attitude within you—one that teaches you to care more about others and their needs than for yourself.

Don't Forget It 👉 *(answers on page 121)*

1. Good leaders must be committed to _____ character.

2. A good leader puts aside his own needs and desires in order to _____ others.

3. Good leaders are willing to _____.

4. I should not desire to be a leader in order for other people to _____ me, but for the purpose of being used by God.

Further Study 📖

Study the example of Jesus in John 13. Knowing He was about to die, Jesus had reason to be depressed and worried about what He would suffer. In the midst of these difficult hours, when He could have been lost in thought, concentrating on His own life, Jesus instead got up and washed the disciples' dirty feet. Think of some people you know who have gone through difficult times but have continued to serve and bless others in the midst of it. They stand out as remarkable people because they reach out to others despite their own hardship. This comes from an inward security in God, knowing that He is good and He has a plan in all of life's circumstances.

Take special note of John 13:3. This was the key for Jesus' security about what was happening in His life. He knew that He had come from God, belonged to God and that He would be with His Father soon. Confidence about His future helped Jesus not only endure the agony of suffering, but also *get up and bless others in the midst of it.* Jesus then gave specific instruction about His example in verses 13–17. He said He gave them this example to follow and that they would be blessed, or happy, if they would *do* the same. It is easy to agree with the concept of serving; it is another thing to actually do it. The key to real satisfaction in life is to serve others. In Acts 20:35 Jesus is quoted as saying, "It is more blessed to give than to receive." Again, happiness comes in giving, not in getting from others. What can you do this week to test this principle?

Other verses about leadership include 1 Kings 3:9, Psalm 101:2, Proverbs 11:3 and 27:23, Zechariah 8:16, Matthew 5:13–16, John 7:24, 1 Timothy 3:4, Titus 2:7–8, 1 Peter 2:21–24 and 5:2–3.

Notes

"For in him we live and move
and have our being." Acts 17:28

Solitude

"Let the morning bring me word of your unfailing love, for I have put my trust in you.
Show me the way I should go, for to you I lift up my soul."
Psalm 143:8

He hadn't even seen it coming. Not much could have prepared him for this moment, yet it would have been helpful to have had some inkling that danger was so near. He had been so focused on making himself and his men ready for the king that he didn't realize that their wives and children had been left vulnerable. David and his 600 men had reported for duty to the Philistine army in a nearby town. While they were gone, the Amalekites had raided his town of Ziklag, burned it and carried off all their women and children. They bitterly blamed David for their troubles and were ready to kill him. What should David do now? How could he possibly defend himself against 600 men? David was shaken, upset over the whole mess and distressed over his men's plan against him.

Making the best decisions takes time, effort and energy.

First Samuel 30 tells this story and shows how David perfectly handled the situation. "But David strengthened himself in the LORD his God" (v. 6, NKJV). Rather than try to talk his way out of the mess or pitch a plan to counterattack, David understood that only God could help him with this problem. He needed specific directions. David chose the right approach: *he went away alone to find out what God wanted him to do, no matter how long it took to hear from God.* "Wait a minute," you say, "who has time for that? David needed action and he needed it right away!"

We live in a fast-food, fast-paced world. No one wants to wait in line, to wait on the phone, to wait to be served. Unfortunately, this impatience has also caused an attitude of not wanting to wait on the Lord. Many decisions need time and prayer before action is taken, but sometimes people just won't wait. This causes them to make mistakes and get hurt in many situations. The fact is that making the best decisions takes time, effort and energy. The main ingredient is time. There is no indication of how long David spent alone with God; what matters is that he did it. He took time alone and wouldn't have moved on without having an answer from God. There was no quick fix to this dilemma.

Life can seem crazy and situations can get out of hand, leaving you frustrated or angry. In these times you need to pull away and get God's help and perspective on what's happening in your life. Hebrews 4:16 says to go "boldly" before God to receive help in time of need (NKJV). David

received instructions from the Lord and followed them, and his men got their families and possessions back. Nothing was missing (1 Samuel 30:19)!

Time alone with God, or personal devotions, is necessary for keeping the right focus in life. God has a plan for each of your days. He has people lined up for you to spend time with. He wants you to bless those people and be His hand of love and help toward them. You know that it isn't natural to put aside your own plans so that you can help someone else. That's why you need time alone with God so that He can remind you of this. Your time alone with God, aside from church, youth group or family devotions, will be important for developing a personal relationship with God that is your own.

If you are going to live for God, then it is important that you know what He wants for you. That means *spending time reading the Bible* and getting to know God through His Word. It also means *spending time in prayer*. Prayer includes thanking God for His goodness, praising and worshiping God for His greatness, and asking God's help for yourself, your family and your friends. But prayer is also about receiving direction for your life each day. It is important to listen to the thoughts God puts on your heart—even writing those thoughts down will help you. This is one way of finding direction from God. Really, prayer is getting your heart "in tune" with God's heart. The more you keep a running conversation going with God throughout the day, the more in tune, or on track, you will be. "Pray continually" (1 Thessalonians 5:17).

Take time every day to read the Bible. Peter told his readers to "grow in the grace and knowledge of our Lord and Savior Jesus Christ" (2 Peter 3:18). There's no getting around it: this takes time. Even a few minutes a day will make a big difference in your life. It also will help you to develop "a spiritual appetite" for God and His purpose for you. You develop an appetite for the things you are eating. If you are eating lots of desserts, you will keep craving desserts with every meal. If you are eating potato chips every day after school, guess what? You will crave chips every afternoon because they have become a habit. Appetites for specific foods are developed through frequent, small tastes. The more you eat a certain food, the more your appetite increases for it.

"Eating" daily of God's Word is a good habit to develop. Paul scolded the Corinthian church for being babies, only able to handle "milk." He said that they ought to be able to handle the "meaty" (or deeper) things of the Word of God (1 Corinthians 3:2 and Hebrews 5:12–14).

You can't always control your daily schedule, but you might get up a little earlier each morning so that you can have time with God at the beginning of the day. Start by giving yourself "small meals" from the Bible and see how you begin to crave more. God will honor your commitment and cause you to want more of Him as you do your part. Jeremiah said, "When your words came, I ate them; they were my joy and my heart's delight" (Jeremiah 15:16). Do you have a daily hunger for God's Word? If reading the Bible is new to you, try small bites at a time and see how God increases your spiritual appetite. Memorizing verses is also important. The psalmist said that keeping God's Word hidden in his heart was the key to staying out of sin (Psalm 119:11). Start a little at a time, and see what a difference it makes to have your mind and heart filled with excellent and helpful truths.

"You will show me the path of life; *in Your presence* is fullness of joy; at Your right hand are pleasures forevermore" (Psalm 16:11, NKJV).

Don't Forget It 👉 *(answers on page 121)*

1. Finding God's direction in my day requires that I spend _____ with Him.

2. I will develop a healthy _____ for God's Word as I read it every day.

3. It is important that I learn to _____ to God in my prayer time.

Further Study

It's important to realize that Jesus also needed time alone to pray and seek direction from His Father. Luke 5:16 says that Jesus "often withdrew to lonely places and prayed." Luke 6:12 says that Jesus spent an entire night in prayer. Many other references to Jesus' prayer life indicate that this was a regular habit for Him, including Luke 22:41, John 6:15 and John 17.

Look specifically at Mark 1:35–39. Jesus got up early while it was still dark and went to a "solitary" place, a place of quiet, a place without distraction. This was evidently His time for receiving instruction from His Father, as you see from the interaction with the disciples that followed. The disciples thought that Jesus was supposed to come back to the same town they had been in because "everyone" was looking for Him. Jesus' answer probably surprised them. Rather than go where *people* wanted Him, Jesus went to the next town to preach because that was where *God* wanted Him to go that day.

King Hezekiah's story in Isaiah 37 is another fantastic illustration of taking a crisis to God. He received threats that Israel would be taken over by its Assyrian enemy, King Sennacherib, who had already done much damage to other nations in the area. Hezekiah could have immediately gathered his troops and headed out offensively, but instead, he took the threatening letter to the temple, laid it out before God and asked for direction and help. Read the end of the chapter and see how the Lord sent His angel, in response to Hezekiah's plea, to fight the battle for him. Hezekiah would have missed this miracle if he had gone out immediately in his own strength. He likely would have lost many of his soldiers and perhaps have been killed himself.

The New Covenant promise of the Old Testament was that God would give the Holy Spirit to each believer. It is through His Holy Spirit that God writes His will upon your heart (Jeremiah 31:33). That means He tells you what to do (see also Jeremiah 33:3 and Hebrews 8:10–11).

Look up these verses about calling out to the Lord for direction and meditating on Him: Psalm 1:2, 4:4, 19:14, 51:4, 10, 116:1–2, 119:14–16, 139:23–24 and 145:18–19, James 1:5–7 and 1 Peter 3:12.

Acts 17:28 says that in God "we live and move and have our being." Pray about everything and in everything: happy times, sad times, hard times and uncertain times. Pray for your school, teachers and administrators. Your prayers for your friends make a great difference—you are intervening in their lives with the hand of God! Don't be going too fast or get too busy in life to talk with your Father in heaven. Life gets confusing and overwhelming. Slow down, and above all *enjoy* what God is doing in your life.

Notes

Become an observer of
the people around you.

Ideals

"'Learn from Me, for I am gentle and humble in heart.'"
Matthew 11:29

"Therefore be followers of God as dear children. And walk in love,
as Christ also has loved us and given Himself for us."
Ephesians 5:1–2 (NKJV)

Everyone has someone whom he looks up to and admires. Who is it you want to grow up to be like? Why do you want to be like that person? Some people dream of following in the steps of a famous athlete or musician. Others want to be in the top ranks of the business world or be a great scientist, making new discoveries. But generally, there are guys around you whom you admire and like because of their good character. An "ideal" is a picture in your mind of someone or something that is nearly perfect. As you grow up, it's important that you have a picture in your mind of what you want to become. Often, this picture will come from picking good qualities you have seen in different men around you.

An "ideal" is a picture in your mind of someone or something that is nearly perfect.

Godly ideals and goals are important. Paul told the Corinthian church to follow his example as he followed the example of Christ (1 Corinthians 11:1). Paul was living in such a way that he could confidently tell people this. That's because his greatest desire was that Jesus would be magnified (shown to others in a big way) through him—whether by death or by life. If Paul died for Jesus, that would be his greatest gain and Jesus would shine through his martyr's death; but if he remained alive, he would keep living for Christ. He wrote this in Philippians 1 while he was under arrest and his future was uncertain. Paul's words and actions were consistent. He lived for Jesus continually by helping people wherever he went. Paul also viewed life's hardships and the suffering he endured as minor compared with his security in Jesus.

Many other character qualities in Paul make him an ideal model to follow after. They include his self-sacrifice, his focus on evangelism, his love for those he discipled, his persistence despite difficulties and his ability to encourage fellow believers. His unshakable faith earned the trust of others so that they could follow his example.

Maybe there is a youth pastor, teacher, coach or missionary you really like. He probably catches your attention because he lives for Jesus, not for himself. It is important for you to be aware of the examples lived out before you. Watch people around you and look for godly qualities in them that you want to incorporate into your life. Then ask God to work these into your life, and begin to practice those qualities in the way you live. It takes diligence, but the right ideals are worth working for and will pay off in your life.

You've probably heard a coach or teacher say that achieving good things is hard work. That's just the way it is. The writer to the Hebrews told them not to become lazy but instead to imitate the godly believers who had lived before them (Hebrews 6:11–12). The writer was telling them to follow after those who had lived as good examples in the faith. The Old Testament is full of real stories of men who have walked before you. Many of these men are examples you will want to study and follow in the way they lived. Others are ones you can learn from who failed in one way or another. Their stories provide warnings about how not to live.

Become an observer of the people around you and a student of Bible characters. Take note of the qualities you like and begin to imitate them, as Hebrews says. This is character development—it is a process of learning and growing. Once these qualities are yours, no one will be able to take them away from you. In fact, you will become someone others can look to as an example. Did you know that the guys you spend time with are already watching you? These years are the perfect time for you to begin setting the ideal example!

Don't Forget It 👉 *(answers on page 121)*

1. It is important for me to have a picture in my mind of what I want to _____.

2. I need to be an observer and find _____ of godliness in the lives of people around

    me.

3. When I see examples of godliness, I can begin to put them in my life through _____.

Further Study

Following the example of others who are godly is a biblical concept. The disciples followed Jesus to learn more about God and godliness. Timothy closely followed Paul as a way of learning the practical demonstration of Christian faith. Paul was a mentor, or teacher, to Timothy. This meant that Timothy watched Paul very closely and had a relationship with Paul that provided counsel, guidance, instruction and training. A pastor once said that every person should have a "Paul" (a teacher to learn from) and a "Timothy" (someone newer to the Christian faith whom you can help). Find someone in your life who is doing well, stick close beside him, and learn from him. Also, become a friend to someone newer in his faith and encourage and help him. This will bring a good balance to your life.

Elijah was a mentor to many young prophets, but one young man in particular stuck closely to him. That man was Elisha. Read his story in 2 Kings 2. Elijah knew it was time to leave this earth and he planned to travel to his departure place alone. Three times Elijah asked Elisha to remain at a certain spot, and all three times Elisha refused. Elisha wanted to see this big event, perhaps thinking he might have a glimpse of heaven. Recognizing the special anointing of God's Spirit upon Elijah, Elisha also wanted every bit of time possible with Elijah. When Elijah asked what he wanted, Elisha responded with great wisdom. Elisha wanted a double portion of the spirit that was within Elijah. Elisha did not want this for his own benefit, to make him greater than the other prophets. Instead, he had a deep spiritual understanding that God was with Elijah. He didn't want just a little of God's Spirit and power; he wanted a "double portion" because he knew only God could bless his work and give him a meaningful ministry. Elisha had learned from Elijah that God's gifts were to be used to bless God's people. Elijah had been an "ideal" man in Elisha's life, and Elisha wisely studied this man's ministry and life *for his own personal growth.*

God has given you parents as the beginning point of study. They are not perfect and will make mistakes, but they are setting examples for you to follow in the way they live, in their own walk with God. Ask them questions and find out about the life lessons they have learned and the experiences they have had. As you grow older, you also should watch the lives of other Christians you know and take note of some of their qualities you want to add to your life.

Notes

Reaching your goals requires a mind to work.

Ambition

"So we built the wall, and the entire wall was joined together . . . , for the people had a mind to work."

Nehemiah 4:6 (NKJV)

No one thought he'd amount to much. He was so slow at everything. It seemed like every project took him twice as long as everyone else. His teachers labeled him dull of mind and gave him little encouragement. In reality, this young man was a very determined and persistent worker. He had high standards and would only turn in his very best work. What others thought was laziness and inability as a 13-year-old was really diligence and excellence. The story of the legendary and brilliant chemist Louis Pasteur is encouraging to those who don't yet know what their goals are but need to have determination and ambition in their daily tasks.

Once teachers began to recognize his potential, they encouraged Pasteur to attend a prestigious private high school. In his studies, Pasteur found math to be very difficult. Rather than avoid it or quit, however, he charged straight ahead and actually volunteered to teach math to younger students. His ambition to conquer his difficulties forced Pasteur to repeatedly study math until he could explain it to new students. It helped him to master this difficult subject before going on to study chemistry.

He worked his very best at what was put before him and learned to reach goals one step at a time.

In a time where many people thought that the study of science would conflict with religious beliefs, Pasteur claimed that science actually brought man nearer to God. He had a solid faith in God and also understood the principle of doing his work with all his heart, for the glory of God. This kept him from running away from difficulties. Pasteur didn't know until many years later that he would want to pursue a career in chemistry, which would require tremendous diligence and perseverance. He just worked his very best at what was put before him and learned to reach goals one step at a time.

You may know Louis Pasteur as the one who discovered that germs spoil food and cause disease. (His name is where the term "pasteurized" milk comes from—milk that is safe to drink, free of the germs discovered by Pasteur.) He also conquered rabies by developing a vaccine for it. Pasteur loved the challenge of solving mysteries and helping people, whether it was finding the cause of illness in farm animals or in humans. He was not ambitious to become famous or rich; he was ambitious to please God by doing all his work to the best of his ability. This is the right kind of ambition.

Nehemiah 4:6 (printed at the beginning of this section) speaks of having a "mind to work." This is the foundation for accomplishing whatever it is you desire. Goals and ideals are wonderful, but they mean very little if you do nothing with them. Do you want to go to college? Do you want to start a business someday? Do you see yourself in full-time ministry? These are great goals, but reaching them requires "a mind to work."

The story of Nehemiah and the families who helped him is a great example of ambition and goals that succeeded with God's help. After being captured by the Babylonians, the Jewish people had been out of their country for 70 years. Some Jews had recently returned to Jerusalem and rebuilt the temple, which had been destroyed so many years ago. Nehemiah was in service to the king of Persia, yet he had a goal in his heart to see the city of Jerusalem protected and fortified, or built up. Jerusalem previously had a thick wall of protection around it, but it was now in ruins. Surprisingly, the king granted permission to Nehemiah to go back to Jerusalem and gather Jews to build up the wall. When Nehemiah got to Jerusalem, he let people know his vision for the city and they agreed to help in the work. "A mind to work" was the determination they needed to accomplish their goal because they had many enemies who tried to prevent them from succeeding.

Nehemiah's story is an important one for you to remember. Sometimes you feel discouraged or your goal seems impossible to reach. There are also times when you want to accomplish something, but it seems like others are against you and wearing you down. This happened to Nehemiah and the families working with him many times. They had real enemies trying to prevent them from building the wall. Each time, Nehemiah looked to God for help and strength. "Strengthen my hands" was his prayer (Nehemiah 6:9).

Keep praying about your desires and determine to do your part in making them happen. Putting your ambitious mind to work will help you reach your goals and keep the enemy of discouragement in check. At times God may change your direction or reshape your goals as you stay close to Him. In John 15:5, Jesus said that you can do nothing without Him. You will need to pray each step of the way in reaching your goals.

As you can see, once you establish some of your ideals and goals, you need ambition, or eager desire and energy, to make them happen. Your goals aren't just handed to you; reaching them comes through hard work. The apostle Paul had many desires and goals in his ministry. One of his passionate desires was to see new Christians grow in their faith. Paul achieved this goal by teaching new believers and writing letters of encouragement and instruction to them. This required hard work and time. In the end, Paul enjoyed the satisfaction of knowing he had labored well and accomplished the purposes God had for him.

The Bible gives warnings about the wrong kind of ambition. Philippians 2:3 says to "do nothing out of selfish ambition or vain conceit," which is pride or self-admiration. Haman is an example of a man who thought too much of himself and thought everyone should admire him. (You'll want to read his story in Esther 3–7.) Haman would do anything to reach his goal. His goal of being second to the king wasn't necessarily wrong; it was *how* he went about it. Wanting the praise of people was his downfall. This is important. *Your goals should not be so important that you are willing to run over people, hurt others, compromise the truth or cheat to get what you want.* Haman's selfish ambition killed him.

Prayerfully set your goals and ideals and then go after them in a right way, with integrity, patience and persistence. Your greatest goal, deserving the greatest amount of energy, should be to please God. He will bless your "mind to work" by giving you strength and direction each step along the way.

Don't Forget It 🖝 *(answers on page 121)*

1. Reaching my goals requires a mind to work, or _____.

2. A great enemy to ambition is _____.

3. The right kind of ambition seeks to please _____ first.

4. I must not hurt others or compromise the _____ to reach my goals.

Further Study

Another goal Paul had in Romans 15:20 was to preach the Gospel in places where no one had already done so. This was a worthy goal that required much ambition and energy to accomplish. Paul's many missionary journeys were the result of this goal. Look up 1 Thessalonians 4:11–12 and consider one outcome of godly ambition: winning the respect of outsiders (non-believers).

James 3:16 says that where envy and selfish ambition are, there is disorder and every evil practice. If a person's ambition is to exalt, or lift up, himself, there will be trouble. This happened with Absalom in 2 Samuel 15–18. His selfish ambition led him to try to take over his father's place in the kingdom. Absalom was so *stuck on* himself that he died after being *stuck up* by his hair, in which he had great pride. There is a price to be paid for selfish ambition. It always leads to problems, and in Absalom's case it ultimately led to his death. Keep praying about your goals and ask God to keep you from selfish ambition.

Notes

_____

_____

_____

_____

_____

_____

_____

_____

_____

_____

It takes self-control to put personal desires aside and treat others as if they are more important than yourself.

Humility

*"'This is the one I esteem: he who is humble
and contrite in spirit, and trembles at my word.'"*
Isaiah 66:2

*"Everything he does is right and all his ways are just.
And those who walk in pride he is able to humble."*
Daniel 4:37

He ate grass with the beasts of the field. His hair was like the feathers of an eagle, and his nails like a bird's claws. The last words he spoke as a human were, "Is not this great Babylon, that I have built for a royal dwelling by *my* mighty power and for the honor of *my* majesty?" As soon as the words were out of his mouth, Nebuchadnezzar was immediately transformed into a wild beast and lived in the fields for the next seven years. Why? Because he was full of pride and self-sufficiency. God had warned Nebuchadnezzar in a dream to turn away from his sin and acknowledge Him. Daniel had interpreted that dream for Nebuchadnezzar and given him the accompanying message, but Nebuchadnezzar ignored it (see Daniel 4).

The best way to achieve your desires is to follow Jesus' example.

Nebuchadnezzar learned the lesson of Proverbs 16:18, which says, "Pride goes before destruction, a haughty spirit before a fall." Nebuchadnezzar was "full of himself." He was a proud man who thought that *he* had made his nation great. In refusing to humble himself before God, Nebuchadnezzar chose to learn the hard way and he suffered great loss personally. He didn't acknowledge that it was God who had blessed him even after seeing His great power demonstrated through Shadrach, Meshach and Abednego in the fiery furnace.

At the end of this seven-year curse, Nebuchadnezzar lifted his eyes up to heaven, acknowledging God, and in doing so his reason and understanding came back to him. Nebuchadnezzar was restored and then made a declaration of the greatness of God: "his ways are just" (Daniel 4:37). That is the message for all people. God's ways are right and they work. The best way to achieve your desires is to follow Jesus' example. Pray through your "wants," then surrender your will and humbly say, "Yet not as I will, but as you will" (Matthew 26:39). This is true humility.

A lot of people think that humility is weakness. Some people think that being humble means you are a weak, quiet person with no ability to make good decisions. They mistakenly think it's

not cool to be humble. In reality, *humility requires great strength and self-control.* All people deal with pride, which is feeling more important or better than others. It takes self-control to put personal desires aside and treat others as if they were more important than yourself.

True humility is the opposite of pride. Pride brags in personal strength and knowledge. Humility recognizes that everything comes from God and that He is in control. Many people don't want to admit that God is the source of all good things (James 1:17). They would rather think that they have the control to make things happen and that they have "earned" all the good things they have.

It's not easy to tell if you possess the quality of humility until you are tested. It isn't until you come up against a challenge or a situation with which you disagree that you know if you are humble or prideful. This is like a mirror revealing what you are really like. It shows either your maturity or your need for growth. What is your reaction, for example, when your parents tell you they believe a certain movie is not appropriate for Christians to see or set a curfew you think is too early? Do you think you know better? Do you argue because you don't want to be left out of your group of friends who are going to see that show? This is a test of humility for you.

These kinds of situations are for your good. Some of them are for you to learn humility in accepting authority and leadership from others. The world is in rebellion against authority. You hear pride and rebellion frequently in questions and statements like, "Who are you to tell me what to do?" "That's so dumb! I know better and I can do whatever I want," or, "I don't care what they say, I'm going there anyway!" Unfortunately, guys who talk like this don't understand that receiving instruction and direction from those in authority is how they are to learn to receive instruction and direction from God: in humility, with acceptance and with a will to obey. Pride is also clearly seen when a person refuses to consider the other side in a disagreement or insists on having the last word.

When you don't like a decision that's been made for you or something seems unfair, that is a chance for you to understand the bigger picture of what is happening. *The key to humility is faith,* which is a complete trust in God. He knows what is happening and He works for your good. There will be many circumstances in your life for which you don't have understanding at that moment. You might say, "Lord, You brought me *here*—is this really best?" Some of these situations may not make sense until years later. In the process, however, you are to believe that God loves you and He has a good plan for your life (Jeremiah 29:11 and Romans 8:28–32). Many of the hard circumstances He allows in your life are for your protection or your growth.

Jesus' example of humble submission to His Father was of great importance to all people. If Jesus had not chosen to surrender His life, salvation would not be available to anyone. Philippians 2:1–8 gives the key to humility through Jesus' example. Verses 1–4 urge you to have a humble mind by thinking of others as better than yourself. Then, verses 5–8 explain that Jesus wasn't trying to be equal with God, but rather made Himself "nothing," or of *no reputation*. Jesus wasn't trying to create an image for Himself, nor was He trying to gain a reputation for greatness. He was simply walking in obedience to His Father, humbly doing the work of His Father by loving and serving the people around Him.

Make it your prayer to be of "no reputation." Psalm 75:7 says, "It is God who judges: he brings one down, he exalts another." Proverbs 21:1 says that God is in control of even the king. God turns the heart of a king wherever He wants it to go, just as He directs the rivers of water. That means that God sees all and is working for the good of all people. He is the One who lifts people up at the right time, whether in your school, church or on your sports team. He is also the One who brings down, or humbles, people. Let Him decide when and how to lift up one person and when to humble another.

This is true humility: letting God have His way in your life and trusting Him to work out the details.

This is true humility: letting God have His way in your life and trusting Him to work out the details. *Your reaction to your circumstance is far more important than the circumstance itself.* Agreeing that God is in control will calm your reactions to a situation you don't like. So many people are angry at life (or at God) because they want to be in control of everything and believe that it is their job to get the best position or take care of a wrong done to them. Uncontrolled anger is everywhere. It comes from prideful demands to be in control of everything. Humility brings you back to God and helps you trust Him with your whole life.

"A man's pride will bring him low, but the humble in spirit will retain honor" (Proverbs 29:23, NKJV).

Don't Forget It 👉 *(answers on page 121)*

1. Humility is _____ _____ under self-control.

2. My response to challenges, disagreements or trials shows if I have _____.

3. I must _____ God in order to accept the events of my life.

4. True humility is letting God have _____ _____ with my life.

Further Study 📖

Colossians 3:12 says to "clothe" yourself with the godly qualities of compassion, kindness, humility, gentleness and peace. Humility is not naturally within you. It comes from a *continual choice* to build it into your life. This takes practice. Most likely you have experienced times where your pride, or "self-promotion," has been obvious to others. After this happens you feel humiliated. This is actually a good thing. It is an opportunity for you to refocus your life and purpose and give yourself back to God in a new way. At other times you might want to be noticed by leaders or friends for some accomplishment. If it goes unnoticed, remember that God is watching you and it must not be the right time for you to be in the spotlight. He will exalt you at the proper time. That's the promise of James 4:6–7, 10.

Most of the time it is pride that causes us to sin and keeps us from doing well. That is why God declared in 2 Chronicles 7:14, "If My people, who are called by My name, will humble themselves, and pray and seek My face, and turn from their wicked ways, then I will hear from heaven, and will forgive their sin and heal their land" (NKJV). Humbling yourself by confessing the sin of pride not only to yourself personally but to God will do much to heal your soul and bring new vision and direction for life.

David's response when he was confronted with his sin in 2 Samuel 12 is significant. It was likely very embarrassing for David to have his sin exposed, but it was also healing for him. In Psalm 32:3, David said that he was wasting away when he kept silent about his sin and wouldn't confess it (because of pride). Psalm 51 is David's humble response to the forgiveness of God. Don't let yourself be condemned in your heart and mind when your pride has been obvious to others or caused you to sin. Confess it right away.

Remember that God sometimes uses other people to show us our flaws and sin. Sometimes you will be confronted by a teacher, a coach, a pastor or your parents. Receive this correction in humility and pray about it, even when you feel like arguing or defending yourself. Allow God's Spirit to convict you, quickly confess it to God in prayer, and receive forgiveness. This healing helps you move on in a spirit of humility. God says He guides and teaches the humble His way (Psalm 25:9). *Humility makes you teachable, ready and willing to learn and grow.*

Look up and meditate on these other passages about humility: Psalm 18:27, 119:21, 147:6 and 149:4, Ecclesiastes 7:9, Isaiah 23:9 and 66:2, Micah 6:8, Matthew 18:4 and 23:12, 1 Peter 3:8 and 5:5–6.

Notes

God wants to build you up and help you during the times when nothing seems to be going your way.

Valleys

"This is what the LORD says: 'Because the Arameans think the LORD is a god of the hills and not a god of the valleys, I will deliver this vast army in your hands, and you will know that I am the LORD.'"
1 Kings 20:28

Brian was really looking forward to this particular Thanksgiving because he was headed for Lake Tahoe to spend time with cousins whom he hadn't seen in a few years. This trip had been planned for months and the whole family was preparing for it. Just three days before the trip, however, Brian got sick. No one gave it much thought, assuming it to be a common cold. A day later, though, Brian's cold took a turn for the worse. Now it was the day before the trip, and Brian and his parents heard the doctor pronounce, "Pneumonia." What a letdown! Why did this have to happen *now*? Brian's parents did their best to console him and his brother and sister, but it wasn't easy.

The day after they would have left for this trip, a shocking front-page newspaper article caught their attention. There had been a tragic pileup of cars due to thick fog on the interstate about two hours' drive from their house. It involved seven or eight cars and several people were killed. Brian's parents figured out that the time they had planned to leave their house and the time they would have arrived at that spot on the interstate would likely have made them part of that accident! In the middle of frustration over changed plans, God was doing something unseen for Brian's family. He was redirecting the whole family and actually protecting them through Brian's illness.

It's true—life is hard. But, God is good and He is a part of all of life, not just the good times.

Can you recall a time of great disappointment in your life that didn't make sense? Some days are just plain hard. Things don't go your way, and sometimes it seems like everything is against you. There are even some days you'd like to erase from your personal history. It's true—life is hard. But, God is good and He is a part of all of life, not just the good times.

Have you considered the purpose God has for you in the difficult situations in life? What is your reaction when circumstances seem stacked against you? Are you angry with God? Do you think

He has deserted you? Do you wonder if He cares about you? Do you have a certainty about His love for you that keeps you securely trusting in Him even when something happens that seems wrong? God sent comforting words to Israel in the midst of hard times through His prophet Jeremiah: "'For I know the plans I have for you,' declares the LORD, 'plans to prosper you and not to harm you, *plans to give you hope and a future*'" (Jeremiah 29:11). Though hardships were surrounding Israel at the time of this prophecy, God wanted His people to know that He had a definite plan for them that was good.

Many years before this, King Ahab also discovered that God was working for good even in hard times. Ben-Hadad, the king of Aram (Syria) and enemy of Israel, had been asserting his power over Israel. It was common in that day for the more powerful country to raid the weaker country, taking their most valuable possessions and sometimes even their wives and children as a way of keeping control over the weaker country. In this story, Ben-Hadad had taken from Israel all their silver and gold and the "best of [their] wives and children" (1 Kings 20:3). However, Ben-Hadad wanted more. He wanted the best possessions from every house. This was the last straw for King Ahab and he refused. Ben-Hadad came back with serious death threats. King Ahab was a bad king who hadn't followed or respected God, but God sent a prophet to tell him that Israel would be delivered anyway. God helped Israel defeat the Arameans in a battle fought in the mountains.

After losing the battle with Israel in the hill country, the officials of Ben-Hadad convinced him that the reason they lost was because Israel's God was the God of the hills, but He was not the God of the valleys. Ben-Hadad's advisors said they would be able to overpower Israel if they fought in the valley, so they laid out a plan to do this. God sent a prophet to King Ahab again and said that because the Arameans claimed He was not the God of the valleys, He would deliver the Arameans over to Israel. God would prove to everyone in this situation that He was God over all: the exciting mountaintop events of life and the difficult days spent in the valleys.

Many people put down Christians during hard times (the valleys) because they say that God has failed, or deserted, the Christian. They wrongly think that God is only the God of good times, easy times and comfortable living (the mountains). When the valleys of difficulties come, they say, "Where is your all-powerful God now?" This is the most common criticism people have with God.

They ask, "How can a loving God allow this or that horrible thing to happen?" Look in 1 Kings 20 and see what God did for Israel. In the valley, the difficult time of battle against impossible odds, God did even *more* for Israel than He did on the mountaintop. In the hard situations of life, God often is most able to show His power because people can do nothing to fix the situation themselves. They can no longer rely on their own strength for help, which leads them to feel the presence of God in real and new ways.

Second Chronicles 16:9 says that God is actively searching throughout the earth to find those He can lift up, give strength to and support. This is the promise for those whose hearts belong to Him. He wants to build you up and help you in the times when nothing seems to be going your way. When everything seems to fall apart, God says, "This is My moment to help you and show you and your friends who I am." Your enemy, Satan, wants to discourage you and make you think God has failed you. Think about the word *discourage*. *Dis* means "away"; *courage* means "bravery and faith." Satan wants to take away your courage to trust God in a hard situation. He wants your disappointment to pull you down, when in each of those situations God wants to show you His comfort and strength.

The way you handle each struggle is part of your life testimony to "Arameans" (unbelievers) of the greatness of God. When you show that you trust God, people around you see strong character in you. They expect you to be angry or depressed and complain. They know that it isn't natural to trust in God and believe that everything will work out for your best. This is living faith. This is how your friends will see God at work and begin to understand that He is real.

When you face a big disappointment, think back on the faithfulness of God in past situations. This can help you trust Him in current ones. You won't always see or understand why plans get changed or things don't happen the way you want, like Brian's family did in their situation. Lean on the promises of God from His Word when you don't see a purpose in the events of your life. The Bible says that He never sleeps or slumbers (Psalm 121:4). He is watching over you and He will direct your path.

Keep hoping and trusting in God. Hope is defined as the "absolute expectation of coming good." With God on your side, you have everything to hope for (Romans 8:31–32). Be thankful for what is good in your life even in the midst of a struggle. Hang on to the truth that God is in charge. He loves you perfectly and is watching over you.

"Hope does not disappoint us, because God has poured out his love into our hearts by the Holy Spirit, whom he has given us" (Romans 5:5).

Don't Forget It 👉 *(answers on page 121)*

1. Sometimes God's power is shown best in the _____ _____ of life.

2. God declares that He is not just the God of the hills, but also the God of the _____.

3. In trying to make me think God has failed me, Satan wants to take away my

   _____ to face hard situations.

4. Remembering God's _____ in the past helps me deal with problems in

   the present.

Further Study 📖

Read the first two chapters of Job. Satan's argument against Job was just like the statement of the Arameans. Satan was saying that Job loved God only because his life had been made comfortable and easy (Job 1:10). Satan and the Arameans were saying that God was only the God of the hills, the high moments of life that are full of excitement or easy living. But in both of these situations God proved Himself to be God of the valleys of life. Notice that God did not send the hard times and suffering to Job. That came from Satan, but God counted Job *worthy* to handle suffering well and used it to make Job's faith and trust in Him grow stronger.

Whatever difficulty is in your life, remember that God has allowed it. That means He believes you are able to handle the challenge in His strength and He knows you will get through. He wants you to lean on Him in the hard times. This will cause your life to be a showcase through which He can display His glory.

First Corinthians 10:13 promises that God will not allow more than you can handle and that He will provide a way of escape. One of the greatest temptations is to doubt God and His ability to see you through tough times. The Israelites' doubt of God led them to sin by grumbling and complaining against Him continually under the leadership of Moses. Their example was a warning that doubt often leads to the sin of complaining. Don't be known as a complainer. Stand firm in hard times or disappointments and let those times strengthen your faith.

In Matthew 9:24–25, Jesus had to put the "mockers" out of the house before He brought Jairus' daughter back to life. If you are being mocked while in a difficult situation, you will do well to separate yourself from the mockers, lest you begin to doubt God's power to work in your situation. Meditate on Isaiah 43:1–4 as your hope and assurance that God will carry you through the valley.

Notes

Competition
teaches you
perseverance
and discipline.
It causes you
to work hard
at becoming
better.

Competition

"I have fought the good fight, I have finished the race, I have kept the faith."
2 Timothy 4:7

"If anyone competes as an athlete, he does not receive the victor's crown
unless he competes according to the rules."
2 Timothy 2:5

Dressed in his shirt and slacks, a father left the bleachers and jumped right into the waist-deep pool as his son was finishing a 25-meter race. He started slapping the water and screaming at his son, "You didn't finish hard enough! You let them pass you!" Swim coach Melinda Schmitt told this true story to *Sports Illustrated* as one of the experiences that contributed to her decision to quit coaching. This was competition gone bad, competition for the wrong reasons and competition out of control. For some people, winning is everything and losing is devastating and shameful.

Don't skip this chapter if you aren't athletic. There is a lot more to competition than sports, as you can see from the verses above. Your spiritual life is compared to an athletic competition because it is an image all people understand even if they aren't athletes themselves. Running a race is simply an illustration of the endurance, discipline and persistence needed in spiritual life. There is a lot to learn about the right kind of competition and its benefits.

> *Your spiritual life is compared to an athletic competition because it is an image all people understand even if they aren't athletes themselves.*

Competition was seen very early in man's history, soon after man's creation in the Garden of Eden. God is actually the Great Competitor against Satan. In His love, God created each person with a will to choose the direction of his or her affection. Not wanting an earth full of robots, God gives each person the choice of following good or evil, Himself or Satan. He is competing for our hearts even now, and He is doing it in the right way: in patient love, wanting the very best for each individual.

Competition is part of all of life. Paul tells us in 1 Corinthians 9:24 that we should run the race of life to win, competing so that we might obtain the prize. In addition, the right kind of competition is actually good for you. It teaches you perseverance and discipline. It causes you to work hard at becoming better. It can stretch you to new levels that you would not have attained on your own. Good competition teaches you to have right attitudes about yourself and others.

People compete for different reasons—some of them good, others questionable. Some people compete for power over others. Some compete for what they think is a better or more important position. Others compete for a reputation of being cool, while others compete for academic rank. Some compete in athletic events or speech and debate, and some even compete for (or fight over) certain friends. It all comes back to the motive of the heart—learning how to compete in a godly way and asking God for wisdom in knowing in which areas it is appropriate for you to compete.

Whether you aspire to be the best in computer programming, mechanics, business, music or athletics, God is pleased with your resolve to give Him your best and not take the easy way out. Some people have a habit of quitting whenever the going gets tough. It is good to be able to try many things, but it's also important that you find an area in which you will stay and work hard. Quitting in hard times cheats you of the benefit of learning to persevere and grow. And quitting in your spiritual life has serious consequences.

Endurance is the ability to hold up or last, especially under strain or suffering. Those who watched Paul's life might have thought he was going to lose big-time at the game of life. Who could have endured so much? Who could have survived all that came his way? When you look at the list of trials Paul went through, from beatings to shipwrecks, hunger and imprisonment, and even being stoned (2 Corinthians 11:24–33), you might wonder why he didn't give up. Few Americans today have endured even one such injustice as Paul endured, yet he kept going, hurdle after hurdle, pressing on toward the prize (Philippians 3:14). Paul was not flustered, distracted or derailed—driven off track—by these problems, because his goal was eternal (2 Corinthians 4:16–17).

The Bible says God "sends rain on the just and on the unjust" (Matthew 5:45, NKJV). This means that both good and bad things happen to Christians and non-Christians alike. When something happens that seems like a setback, remember that you are competing for an eternal prize. Don't let your enemy (Satan) sidetrack you and stop you. Some guys quit going to church when life gets rough. Some guys quit reading the Bible, quit praying and quit coming to God with their struggles to seek help and direction. This is exactly what Satan wants them to do. The best path, however, is to keep going and never quit at the fundamentals of your Christian walk. God will meet you and help you through the rough spots, and in the process you will experience great growth.

Good competitors are solid in the fundamentals. What are the fundamentals? They are the basic skills, the everyday, repetitive things a beginner would do who is new to a field of interest. For sports, that would mean practicing basic individual skills before competing in a game or match. These fundamental skills require diligence and perseverance and a willingness to repeat them over and over again even when you think you've mastered them. You know that the fundamentals in building your relationship with God come through regular Bible reading, prayer, Bible studies and going to church. These are the foundations of building your spiritual strength and endurance for the events of life.

When the Chicago Bulls won six NBA championships, their coach, Phil Jackson, said that the strength of his team was the players' solid fundamentals. The Bulls, the best of the best during those years, started every practice with time devoted to drills on individual fundamental skills. Coach Jackson said this

Your regular practice of spiritual fundamentals will give you the ability to function well spiritually and keep you from quitting or giving up.

was what gave them the ability to function well under pressure as a team at the end of close games. Your regular practice of spiritual fundamentals will give you the ability to function well spiritually and keep you from quitting or giving up.

For a musician, good fundamentals might mean frequent repetition of beginning techniques, such as practicing scales. In academics, it means learning how to take notes and a commitment to study and memorization. These foundational habits are the basis of becoming better in competition. No one can step right in and be the best without practicing the fundamentals. Mastering the fundamentals carries you through difficult situations that would be more challenging and even scary for someone who has not worked as diligently on the basics. When you watch competition on TV, it is essential to know that hours and hours of work, which weren't "fun," came before the performance. Those who ignore the fundamentals out of laziness or pride usually fail soon after.

What are the fundamentals of Christian truths that are necessary in all forms of competition? It begins with continually (daily) reminding yourself that God has given you your talents and abilities (1 Corinthians 4:7). Even if you have worked hard to develop those gifts, remember that God is the original source of good gifts and your talent comes from Him (James 1:17). Not one person ever chose where he would be born, who his parents would be, how tall he would grow or what talents he would have.

Next, realize that you are responsible to take the talents you have been given and use them well. In Matthew 25, Jesus tells the story of servants who had been given talents by their master. Those who used their talents well were called good and faithful servants and given further gifts and responsibilities. The servant who did not use his talent was called wicked and lazy. God wants you to develop and use your gifts, so don't hide your talent!

Another fundamental is that the Bible makes it clear that your abilities are not to be used only for your own benefit, but also for God's purposes and His kingdom. Romans 6:13 states that your body can be used as an instrument of righteousness for God. Rather than "blowing your own horn" and using your abilities for personal gain and glory, God desires that you use the instrument of your body for good, for righteousness, to bless people in His name, in His way. God gave you gifts to use to bless others around you and give glory to His name, not to exalt yourself.

Using these three fundamental truths of competition (acknowledging your ability is God-given, diligently developing your skills and using your talents for God's purpose) will further your development as a person and help you do well under pressure.

Good competition can make you a better person when you compete for the right reasons and with the right attitude. It is important to compete in an attitude of humility. Many athletes and businessmen are arrogant about their success. They take pride in themselves, as if they made themselves successful on their own. They like being on top. The truth is, there will always be someone better coming around the corner. There will come another who will beat the record time or statistics, and there will come another who will develop better computer technology or have a bigger bank account. If a person is out for only his personal success, jealousy and envy will enter in when another comes along and does better. Being proud over success is not godly. Your success in God's eyes comes in being humble, gracious toward others, encouraging of others and thankful to God for your ability. These qualities of godliness in an athlete, student or businessman are what point watching people toward God.

The best athletes want to compete with those who are tops in their field. They know that they will get better as they compete in difficult situations and against those who are the very best. Roger Bannister, the first man to run a mile in less than four minutes, used this principle. He brought together top runners to race against, knowing it would push him to run his best. He had a personal goal, and he knew that only the best competition would help him achieve his goal. In taking this risk, he once ran side by side against Australia's top runner and they both clocked under four minutes, Bannister winning by one second. This is a biblical concept—being sharpened in skill to become a better person. It works in many areas of life. Proverbs 27:17 says, "As iron sharpens iron, so one man sharpens another." Roger Bannister let the best in his field push him to sharpen his own skills.

Competition also helps you learn a good deal about yourself. Ask yourself the following questions before and after you are involved in a competition. Your answers to them reveal where your heart is. As you grow and mature, you will see progress in the way you can answer them.

1. Can I have success without becoming prideful?

2. Can I deal with losing without becoming angry, discouraged or depressed?

3. How do I respond in stressful situations with many others watching?

4. How do I handle correction from instructors or coaches?

5. How do I respond to injustice if officials' calls or judges' results do not appear to be fair or right?

6. Can I learn to respect my opponents in competition, trying to give my best while giving them credit for their efforts?

7. Can I acknowledge that the ability others have is also given to them by God and thank Him for that?

8. Can I learn to give glory to God, thanking Him *in* all things, even if not always *for* all things (1 Thessalonians 5:18)?

Keep asking yourself these questions as you compete, and keep the faith as you compete! Jesus did not give up in His competition against Satan on the cross. To all onlookers, it looked like Satan had won, but Jesus gained the victory in the "third overtime"!

"'He who glories, let him glory in the LORD'" (2 Corinthians 10:17, NKJV).

Don't Forget It 🖝 *(answers on page 121)*

1. Competition teaches me about endurance, _____ and persistence.

2. God gave me my gifts to use to give _____ to Him, not to exalt myself.

3. Continual practice of the basic _____ will make me a better competitor.

4. It is important to compete in an attitude of _____.

Further Study

"To whom much is given, much is required." This concept comes from Luke 12:48. Think about the responsibilities that come with success in any kind of competition. Greed and money are powerful influences over people. Every once in a while, stories emerge of athletes who have accepted money to "throw" a game or guarantee a specific point spread. Similar scandals take place regularly in business for power and position. A solid character is necessary to resist these temptations. A commitment to rightness is needed. First Timothy 1:18–19 says to "fight the good fight," having faith and a good conscience. This passage goes on to say that those who have rejected this teaching have "shipwrecked their faith." The approval of God is most important in any success, and a good conscience is essential to proper competition. Fix your eyes on Jesus, the "author and perfecter" of your faith, as you run your race in life with endurance (Hebrews 12:1–2).

Study Jonathon's story in 1 Samuel 19–20. According to tradition, Jonathon should have been the next king after his father, Saul. But God had chosen and anointed David as the next king. Jonathon could have been jealous, angry or full of self-pity. Instead, Jonathon came alongside David, befriended him and became a help and encouragement to David. Rather than compete for the kingship, Jonathon protected David's place as king. There will be times where the Lord calls you to be an encourager of someone else's success. Learn to be happy for others who are "chosen" to be the star and support them even as you are working on your own talent or skill.

Notes

_____

_____

_____

_____

_____

_____

The best preparation for tomorrow is to do today's work superbly well.

Faithfulness

*"'Well done, good and faithful servant! You have been faithful with a few things;
I will put you in charge of many things. Come and share your master's happiness!'"*
Matthew 25:21

Seventeen-year-old Drew had just been hired as a stocker at a new supermarket. He jumped in with all his heart, working harder and faster than all the others and taking on other jobs during the slow times. His supervisor was impressed with this young man and began to watch him closely, thinking he could eventually promote Drew. Over a period of weeks, however, Drew became friends with another young employee who liked to talk and didn't put out extra effort. Drew began to relax and get comfortable on the job, looking forward to working with his new friend. He began to talk back and forth across the aisle in slow times instead of looking for extra work.

There are a lot of times when everyday work seems boring and unimportant.

Months later when Drew was having a conversation with his supervisor, he was told that he had been a candidate for training new employees. However, he was no longer in the running for the job now because he wasn't performing as strongly as he had in the beginning. It was too late for Drew with this employer, but he learned an important lesson for the next job he took when he went on to college. There would be no more slacking off for him. He was disappointed in himself that he had not kept a high standard and been a light for Jesus to those around him at his job.

There are a lot of times when everyday work seems boring and unimportant. Some of it may even seem useless and unnecessary. When you stop and think about it, however, you realize that the little jobs are a part of learning and growing so that later in life you can handle the big jobs that will be required of you. Aren't you glad you weren't required to go to a 40-hour-a-week job as a four-year-old? You have been able to take on new responsibilities a little at a time as you've developed. It's hard to see that as a privilege, isn't it? Remember, even though you don't really know where you'll be in a few years in your first job or in your life career, *the way you handle your current jobs may determine the path you take in the future*. That is the message of Matthew 25:21.

Sir William Osler, one of the most brilliant physicians ever, taught young doctors in Canada, England and the United States and changed the way medical training was accomplished world-wide. Dr. Osler was continually telling young men interested in the medical profession that "the best preparation for tomorrow is to do today's work superbly well."

When you mow the lawn, do you clean up after yourself, or just do the job quickly to get it over with so you can go play? Do you complete just the bare minimum in your schoolwork, enough to get by, or do all that you know you can do in order to succeed and learn as much as you can? Do you stuff things under your bed when it's time to clean your room, or do you put games and books away where they belong? Do you fold your clothes neatly so that they'll wear well when you get them out, or do you throw them in your drawer without caring about them? The way you approach everyday tasks affects your ability to take on more responsibilities. More than that, God has a plan for you and wants you to give your very best in all things (Colossians 3:23). The mark of a job done well and right should be one of the greatest testimonies to others of the difference God makes in your life. It also can cause people to recognize you as a potential leader.

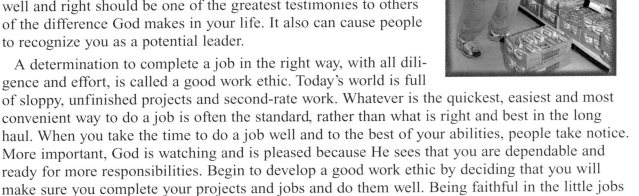

A determination to complete a job in the right way, with all diligence and effort, is called a good work ethic. Today's world is full of sloppy, unfinished projects and second-rate work. Whatever is the quickest, easiest and most convenient way to do a job is often the standard, rather than what is right and best in the long haul. When you take the time to do a job well and to the best of your abilities, people take notice. More important, God is watching and is pleased because He sees that you are dependable and ready for more responsibilities. Begin to develop a good work ethic by deciding that you will make sure you complete your projects and jobs and do them well. Being faithful in the little jobs prepares you for the greater responsibilities that God has planned for you.

Try to grasp the big picture as you look at David's life and see how his faithfulness in each job prepared him for a future he knew nothing about—being the king of Israel. As a boy, David was given the unwanted, unnoticed job of tending sheep. It was a lowly job with no significance. No one will fully know what David did during all that time, but you can conclude that he was a very faithful worker and understood that he was working for God more than for his earthly father. In those fields David learned of God and wrote many songs to Him. There, David also learned that true leadership was risking his life for the good of others. He learned this by shepherding well. He killed a lion and bear while protecting the sheep (1 Samuel 17:36). Many people would have just let the bear or lion have a couple sheep rather than risk their lives. After all, what's a couple sheep from the whole flock? No doubt God was greatly pleased by David's integrity, his determination to work hard while "no one" was watching.

This commitment to excel in his work prepared David for what God had for him next. It was because David worked faithfully in the "little things" that God was able to give him "bigger assignments"—like Goliath! If David had been lazy and negligent in his work out in the fields, it is unlikely that God would have chosen him as the next king of Israel.

Psalm 78:70–72 contains a critical lesson and message. It states that God took David directly from tending the sheep to shepherding the people of Israel. Clearly, *David's work as a young man had a direct purpose in building his future*. This is true for everyone. Ephesians 2:10 says that before you were born, God had specific works planned for you to complete. Look at each day as a day planned by God for you to work for Him. This perspective will bring meaning and purpose into those everyday jobs, as each one builds you up and makes you ready for the next. Remember this the next time you are tempted to grumble about an assignment or job given to you. It has a purpose: to refine you, to make you grow and to prepare you for something bigger later on. No assignment is wasted. God has a purpose in all that He brings your way, and He is not pleased with laziness or sloppiness.

Jesus was ready to go to heaven after *completing* the work God had given Him to do (John 17:4). It was His joy and pleasure to do the work of His Father. Make that your prayer as well!

Don't Forget It 👉 *(answers on page 121)*

1. If I do a complete job in the right way, I have a good _____ _____.

2. My faithfulness in the little jobs prepares me for the _____ _____

   God has for me.

3. God has specific _____ planned for me to complete.

4. My work as a young man has a direct purpose in _____ my future.

Further Study

Joseph is another example of one who was faithful in the "little things." His life was a great example because he worked hard in spite of being treated unfairly. He could have become lazy after being treated wrongly, but he clearly understood that God was in every part of his life and he needed to be responsible wherever he was, in every little job. It was his positive attitude and good work ethic that led to practicing leadership first as a slave in Potiphar's household and later in prison. All this prepared him to be a great leader in Egypt. You can read his story in Genesis 37, 39–50.

Read the parable Jesus told in Matthew 25:14–30 and discuss the different portions of "talent" the lord of the servants gave to each man. Apply this story to your life as you evaluate the possible meanings of "talents," be they monetary or gifts and abilities.

Jesus said He brought glory to God by completing the work that God had given Him to do (John 17:4). Paul was very careful not to take advantage of others by "freeloading" (Acts 20:33–35). Other verses on work and responsibility include Proverbs 18:9 and 22:29, Ecclesiastes 3:22, John 5:17, 1 Corinthians 4:2 and 15:58, Ephesians 6:5–8, 1 Thessalonians 4:11–12 and 2 Thessalonians 3:10.

Notes

Serving
others
is how
you serve
the Lord.

Service

"Serve wholeheartedly, as if you were serving the Lord, not men, because you know that the Lord will reward everyone for whatever good he does, whether he is slave or free."
Ephesians 6:7

The founder of a cleaning company understood that all of his work was service to God. He had a special purpose for his company: he wanted everyone who worked there to know that their work was to be service for the Master, Jesus. He hired only people who understood the vision to make their labor far superior to the average company—not to beat out other companies, but to please God. They worked harder and better than any other cleaning company to please their Master, Jesus, and to be a witness to those who saw their work. This company, ServiceMaster, began in the Chicago area, but expanded across many states because its quality of work was superior to their competitors'. Due to its commitment to good service, ServiceMaster is still going strong after 50 years of business.

Romans 12:1 tells Christians to be "living sacrifices." This means that everything you do, all your "living days," are meant to be service to God. It means giving yourself back to God so He can use you, which is indeed a sacrifice (giving up) of yourself and some of your desires. Really, it is the best way to eliminate selfishness in your life. God knows that His people need to be freed from selfishness because self-centeredness leads to unhappiness and emptiness. He provided the answer to this problem, for it is in serving Him that true happiness is found. By God's design, part of serving Him is done through serving others. Romans 12:1 also says that serving God is one way we worship and honor Him. This is because service helps us forget about our own pleasure and causes us to think about the pleasure of others. In the end, when you sacrificially give up your personal desire by serving someone else, you find that God fills you with more joy than you could imagine. God always gives great satisfaction back to us when we choose to serve Him.

> *Serving God is one way we worship and honor Him.*

Service is also what you do to help someone else. It means that you give of yourself to bless or help another person. It is very rewarding to see the joy on someone's face when you've worked hard on a project for him. Have you ever asked your dad if you could mow the lawn for him?

Have you seen the surprise on his face and the happiness he expressed in having some free time to relax? This is just the beginning of learning to bless others by offering yourself to God in service. There are many places and ways to serve as you grow up.

Unfortunately, service to others has been neglected in our society in recent years. That's why many high schools are now requiring "community service" in order for students to graduate. These programs have been brought into the school system because people are so busy with their own lives that they don't take time to think about the needs of others. Older people who need help often have no one to help them. People do not volunteer to help others or help the community in which they live. Ephesians 6:7 (printed at the beginning of this section) states that your service for others is really the way you serve the Lord. This means that if you are not involved in serving others in some way, you are missing some of the blessing that God has for His children. In serving others, you are a witness to others of God's love.

Your parents may be involved in serving at church with children's classes, helping teachers at school or leading scout clubs. They are allowing God to use them to bless others. This is part of their service to God. They model for you the need to be involved in the lives of others rather than living for personal pleasure. Ask God to open your eyes to see ways that you can be a practical help to other people. A simple task like raking leaves can be a great help to someone unable to do the job. Helping a younger boy learn a skill in a sport is a great encouragement to him and to his parents. The practical help you offer to someone is a gift of service to God.

Some people mistakenly think that service for the Lord has to have a title, like "missions project," "missions trip," "Bible study leader" or "pastor." The ServiceMaster story illustrates the fact that *all* of life is to be service for the Lord, whether you are flipping burgers, bagging groceries, coaching Little League baseball or serving as the president of a corporation. *In all that you do, work as if everything depends on you, but pray as if it all depends on God.* This thinking helps you work for the Lord while you keep the perspective that God is the One who guides you each step of the way and blesses the work of your hands (Psalm 90:17).

You will be working hard on personal goals all through your life. You don't have to wait until you've "perfected" your talents or earned a degree in order for God to use you. You will want to find ways you can help and serve in your church, school or neighborhood all through your growing up years. In doing this, you will please your Master, Jesus, and learn happiness and satisfaction by giving of yourself to bless others.

"'The son of Man did not come to be served, but to serve, and to give his life a ransom for many'" (Matthew 20:28).

Don't Forget It ☛ *(answers on page 121)*

1. Living to serve God is what brings _____ _____ into my life.

2. Serving others helps get rid of _____ in my life.

3. My service for the Lord does not have to have a special _____, like "missions project."

4. A job well done is a _____ to others that I am a Christian.

Further Study ✎

Look at 1 Timothy 3:1–13 and Titus 1:5–9 regarding the qualifications for leaders to serve in the church. All Christian men should desire these qualities whether they work in the church or not. Make a list of these qualities for yourself and write down how you see yourself practicing them now. Pray over this list regularly and ask God to show you how to begin to develop them now as you are growing up. Developing these qualities in your life now will make you more useful to God and better able to serve others.

Notes ✐

_____

_____

_____

_____

Developing your character qualities will help keep you solid in your faith and upright in your living.

Flaws and Failures

"I know that nothing good lives in me, that is, in my sinful nature.
For I have the desire to do what is good, but I cannot carry it out.
For what I do is not the good I want to do; no, the evil I do not want to do—this I keep on doing."
Romans 7:18–19

"One thing I do: Forgetting what is behind and straining toward what is ahead, I press on toward the goal to win the prize for which God has called me heavenward in Christ Jesus."
Philippians 3:13–14

Basketball star David Robinson once said, "Failure doesn't get enough credit. It teaches us humility, perseverance and the value of hard work. When you fail, you have to learn from your mistakes and move on." Failures serve a purpose in helping you grow and mature. You have the potential and the choice to make changes whenever you fail. The apostle Paul chose to forget what was behind him—his failures—and continue steadfastly on his path.

Some people incorrectly believe that humans are born completely "good" and that the wrong environment makes them "bad." The truth is that humanity is drawn to sin. It is human nature to sin, and every person has that natural tendency. As a Christian you are engaged in a battle of the flesh (your old sinful nature) against the spirit (your new nature in Christ). Second Corinthians 5:17 says that anyone who receives Christ becomes a new person and the old things are gone. Even though you are a new person in Christ (that's how God sees you), Satan still wants to pull you down and make you think you will always be a failure and unable to overcome certain temptations. This is the struggle Paul referred to in Romans 7:18–19. He *wanted* to do good but kept finding himself doing poorly and sinning. This struggle goes on inside every Christian. There is a part of you still vulnerable to sin, even though the new heart within you wants to do right and honor God.

There is a part of you still vulnerable to sin, even though the new heart within you wants to do right and honor God.

While every Christian battles sin, each one is a unique individual. Each person has his own sin he struggles with more than another. One guy may view everything in a negative way and allow simple situations to get him down. Another guy who doesn't struggle with this may see a difficulty as a great opportunity to wait and see what God will do to help. This person naturally trusts in God, while the one who is negative takes the burden on himself. It would be good for you to spend some time thinking about what aspects of your faith come easily to you and then evaluate which areas you struggle with. For example, do you have a natural tendency to cover up for your mistakes and lie? Recognizing your weakness is the first step in correcting it. Maybe you easily get jealous of your friend's abilities. You can overcome this by practicing Romans 12:15, which says, "Rejoice with those who rejoice." Showing genuine happiness for your friend's success and encouraging him will help you overcome envy. On the other hand, another person may have trouble with the last part of Romans 12:15, which tells us to show compassion for those who struggle and have difficulties.

Either way, you will benefit from personal evaluation of your strengths and weaknesses regarding the qualities mentioned in this book, as well as more from the Bible. It is good for you to evaluate your progress from time to time to see how you are doing. Progress in one area may lead you to see another area that needs work.

What weaknesses do you see most often in your life? Will you ask God to help you resist those temptations and overcome them? Weaknesses cause you to depend on God even more. Paul said that in his weaknesses he experienced the power of God (2 Corinthians 12:19). Faults and weaknesses make you aware of your need for God. Being aware of your flaws helps you learn to lean on God for strength and teaches you to listen to Him and follow His directions for your life. Your faults also keep you humble before the Lord and before people.

Keep working on your trouble spots and see what a great work God does in and through you. A real "wise guy" will humbly seek God in order to grow and mature. The wise men of the East dropped everything, packed up and went the distance until they found Jesus. You are also becoming a man of wisdom as you seek true wisdom from above, which is "pure, then peaceable, gentle, willing to yield, full of mercy and good fruits, without partiality and without hypocrisy" (James 3:17, NKJV). Remember the promise of 2 Peter 1 from the beginning of the book: you will be fruitful and productive as you diligently work towards godliness every day!

"He who began a good work in you will carry it on to completion until the day of Christ Jesus" (Philippians 1:6).

Don't Forget It 👉 *(answers on page 121)*

1. Evaluating my failures can help me _____ and mature.

2. My weaknesses cause me to _____ to God for strength.

3. My faults keep me _____ before God.

Further Study 📖

Peter was a disciple who understood weaknesses and faults. Jesus had told Peter that he would deny Him on the very morning of the day that it happened. But Jesus also had very comforting words for Peter that would come back to his memory later on. Jesus told Peter that Satan was trying to pull him down, but reassured him with the words, "I have prayed for you" (Luke 22:32). Imagine that! Jesus, knowing what would happen, prayed for Peter and expected him to do well after that failure.

Jesus also told Peter in that verse to strengthen the brothers after he turned back from his failure. That speaks of true repentance: turning from the sin and helping others who struggle. Jesus wasn't done with Peter because he had failed, and He isn't done with you when you fail. If you look at John 21:15–19, you will see Jesus reaching out to Peter again and reaffirming him in ministry. Jesus asked Peter three times if he loved Him, and each time Jesus gave Peter his assignment—to feed His sheep. Jesus was showing Peter the reality of "forgetting what is behind" and moving on to what is next. Peter would grow and mature, having learned from his fall, and eventually die a martyr's death. He died on a cross upside down, declaring himself unworthy to die as Jesus did.

When you need assurance from God that your sins are forgiven, look up these passages: Psalm 25:6–9, 103:12 and 147:3, Jeremiah 31:34 and 1 John 1:9. Keep pressing on toward the prize God has for you!

Notes

ANSWER KEY

Character Building
1. everyday/daily
2. trust
3. useful/fruitful
4. flaws

Obedience
1. obedience
2. faith/trust
3. prideful

Companions
1. right
2. men
3. strong/good
4. servant

Standing Alone
1. living rightly
2. example
3. falling
4. stand out

Knowledge
1. use
2. sin
3. Holy Spirit

Image
1. bless, hurt
2. hear
3. consistent

4. love
5. family
6. Faith
7. back
8. darkness

Leadership
1. good
2. serve/help
3. work
4. notice

Solitude
1. time
2. appetite
3. listen

Ideals
1. become
2. examples
3. practice

Ambition
1. ambition
2. discouragement
3. God
4. truth

Humility
1. great strength
2. humility

3. trust
4. His way

Disappointments
1. hard times
2. valleys
3. courage
4. faithfulness

Competition
1. discipline
2. glory
3. fundamentals
4. humility

Faithfulness
1. work ethic
2. greater responsibility
3. works
4. building

Service
1. true happiness
2. selfishness
3. title
4. witness

Flaws and Failures
1. grow
2. look
3. humble